Housing Rights Guide
2008–09

13th Edition

Geoffrey Randall

**Housing Rights Guide
2008–09**
Geoffrey Randall

13th Edition
ISBN 978 1 903595 73 2

Geoffrey Randall is an independent housing and research consultant with Research and Information Services.

Acknowledgements

Previous editions of this guide have been produced with the advice and help of many people. For this edition I would like to thank in particular Shelter's Legal Services team for checking the text and and Naomi Anders for all her help with the editing and production of the guide.

Published by Shelter
88 Old Street, London EC1V 9HU
0845 458 4590
www.shelter.org.uk

Registered charity number 263710
RH 1021.2

Everyone should have a home
Shelter, the housing and homelessness charity

Contents

Introduction

The *Housing Rights Guide* is a reference book for advisers and for people with housing problems. In addition to an outline of the law, it gives practical guidance on how to resolve problems, and gives essential information on finding, paying for, keeping, and repairing a home.

This new edition has been completely updated to include recent changes in English and Welsh housing law and practice, including: new rights to repairs and improvements for tenants; licensing of houses in multiple occupation and some other private rented homes; new protection for deposits paid by tenants of private landlords; new low-cost ownership; Home Information Packs for home buyers; and new laws against discrimination on the grounds of sexual orientation or faith.

Housing law is complicated. This guide is a starting point for advisers and people who want to check their rights, but if the problem is complicated, visit www.shelter.org.uk/adviceonline or contact Shelter's free housing advice helpline on 0808 800 4444. Advisers who want more information about the law can find it in the publications listed in Useful publications on pages 189–191.

Chapter 1 gives information on finding a home, including rented homes from local councils, housing associations and private landlords; buying a home; and finding temporary and emergency accommodation.

Chapter 2 gives details of the rights of people who are threatened with eviction from their homes, including all types of tenants, owners, people living in mobile homes, and squatters.

Chapter 3 gives information on how to reduce your housing costs and how to seek help with paying for your home. It includes separate sections for private, council, and housing association tenants, for owners, and for people living in hostels.

Chapter 4 gives information on tenants' rights to have repairs and improvements done to their homes, and advice on how to get help with the cost of improvements.

Chapter 5 contains details of the wide range of other rights available to tenants and long leaseholders, whether their landlord is a private owner, the council, or a housing association, including what information landlords must give tenants, what to do if the landlord is harassing you, how much landlords can charge for services, and many other tenants' rights.

Chapter 6 is for people whose marriage, civil partnership, or relationship has broken down, and gives information on rights to stay in the home, and the rights of people suffering from domestic violence.

Chapter 7 gives information on where to go for further advice and help.

The laws described in this guide only apply to England and Wales. Housing law changes fairly frequently; the information here is based on the law at November 2007.

If you have any comments on the guide or suggestions for improvements, please send them to:

Geoffrey Randall
Research and Information Services
48 Castle Street, Eye
Suffolk IP23 7AW

geoffrey@researchservices.org.uk
www.researchservices.org.uk

Finding a home 1

Rent or buy?

Buying a home is only an option for people who can afford the prices in the areas where they want to live. However, even if you can afford to consider buying, it may not always be the best option. The advantages of buying are:

- You may have a choice of properties and areas, depending on the price range you can afford.
- You have a higher degree of control over your home, subject to building and planning regulations.
- You can only normally lose your home if you fail to keep up mortgage payments.
- In the longer term, usually after several years of paying off a mortgage, it can be cheaper than renting.

The disadvantages of buying are:

- The costs in the first few years are usually higher than renting from the local council or a housing association, although they may be lower than renting a similar property from a private landlord.
- The initial cost of buying a home can run to several thousands of pounds, in addition to mortgage repayments.
- You are responsible for all repair and maintenance costs, which can run to hundreds or thousands of pounds a year.
- There is limited, or no help available with your housing costs if your income drops.

The advantages of renting from a local council or housing association are:

- Costs are usually lower than renting in the private sector.
- If your income drops, help is available through housing benefit to pay the rent.
- Most of the repairs and maintenance, apart from minor items, will be carried out by the landlord.
- You will normally only be at risk of losing your home if you fail to pay the rent, cause considerable damage to the property, or cause serious annoyance to your neighbours.
- Local authorities and housing associations are non-profit making and aim to provide a good service to tenants, although this may not always be achieved.

The disadvantages of renting from a local council or housing association are:

- In some areas you may have to wait for months or years before you are offered a home, particularly if you want one of the more popular areas or types of home, for example a house rather than a flat.
- You may have limited or no choice over the area or type of home you are offered.
- You will have less control over your home, for example over making improvements to the property.
- The rent you pay will increase over time and you may end up, after several years, paying more than someone who has bought their home.

The advantages of renting from a private landlord are:

- There may be a wider choice of area and type of property, if you can afford the rent.
- There is unlikely to be a waiting list.
- If your income drops, help is available through housing benefit to pay the rent, although the full rent may not be met.

- Most of the repairs and maintenance, apart from minor items, should be carried out by the landlord, although some private landlords can be bad at carrying out repairs.

The disadvantages of renting from a private landlord are:

- Rents can be very high.

- The rent you pay will increase over time and you may end up, after several years, paying more than someone who has bought their home.

- New tenants only have limited protection from eviction and the landlord can ask for the property back when they want it, although you rarely have to leave immediately.

- You will have less control over your home, for example over making improvements to the property.

By looking in the other sections of the *Housing Rights Guide* you can find out more about the different rights of owners and tenants.

Different types of homes will suit different people. People with stable incomes and who do not want to move for at least three or four years, may be best buying a home, if they can afford it. Local authority or housing association homes are more suitable for families, or older people on fixed or low incomes. Young people who want a home immediately and who only want to stay for a limited time, may be best renting privately.

The following sections give advice on how to go about renting or buying.

Renting from the council

Although the number of council homes to rent has been declining, they are still the main source of affordable rented housing in many areas. This section tells you how to apply for a home. In some areas, some or all of the council housing stock has been passed over to housing associations, but this section also applies to those areas. To avoid repetition it refers to 'the council' throughout.

It is often thought that to get a council house, applicants have to join a long queue. In reality, some people's need for a home is greater, or more urgent, than others', and councils have to take this into account when deciding who should be offered a home first.

In many areas there is a shortage of council housing and there are many more people applying than can be offered a home. In other areas, homes are plentiful, but they may not be the type or in the areas you would prefer.

This section describes how councils decide on their priorities and who has a legal right to housing. Councils must, by law, publish details of how they make these decisions. This is known as their allocation scheme and you have a right to see a copy.

You can find out how to make a housing application from the town hall or local council offices. Their number will be in the telephone directory, or you can find it in a local library. Normally you will receive a form from the council's housing department and will have to give details of yourself, your family, if any, and your present housing conditions.

If you are being actively considered for an offer of housing, you will probably be visited by someone from the council to check on your details.

It is often necessary to re-register each year and when you put your name on the list, you should check when you have to renew your application.

How allocation schemes work

The council cannot prevent you from applying simply because you may not be from the local area. It has to decide whether you fall into one or more of the categories of applicants who must be given reasonable preference, taking into account your housing need. The categories are:

- people who are homeless
- people who are owed a duty by any housing authority under homelessness legislation

- people occupying insanitary or overcrowded housing, or living in other unsatisfactory housing conditions
- people with a need to move on medical or welfare grounds
- people with a need to move to a particular area to avoid hardship to themselves or to others.

If you fall into one or more of these categories, the council's scheme must give you preference over applicants not within these categories. How councils do this is up to them but common schemes include:

- **Points-based schemes**: applicants are awarded points based upon their preference and housing need; those with the most points are offered suitable housing as it becomes available.
- **Banding schemes**: applicants are placed in bands that reflect their preference and housing need. Properties are usually offered to applicants within the highest band first.
- **Choice-based schemes**: all councils should have a choice-based scheme by 2010. All available properties are advertised and applicants are invited to apply for homes of their choice. Where two or more applicants apply for the same property, it is awarded to the applicant with the highest priority. If you are unsuccessful, the council should give you feedback to help you assess your chances of success in future applications.

Where two or more applicants have the same level of priority, the council is entitled to take into account other factors, such as waiting time, local connection with the area, and any outstanding rent arrears. However, this must be clearly set out in the council's allocation scheme.

The council can decide that someone is not eligible for housing if they have been guilty of unacceptable behaviour that would entitle it to evict them if they had been a council tenant. The council must notify you in writing that it has decided you are not eligible, giving reasons for its decision. If you believe you should no longer be treated as ineligible, you can make a fresh housing application.

If you do not agree with any decision about the facts of your application, or a decision that you are not eligible because of your behaviour, you are entitled to ask for a review of the council's decision.

People from abroad

Some people from abroad will not be eligible for housing. This includes many people who are subject to immigration control, asylum seekers, people who are allowed to stay provided they do not claim from public funds, sponsored immigrants who have been in the UK for less than five years, people who fail the habitual residence test for welfare benefits, or many people from the EU who are not working or not family members of EU workers. If the council informs you that you are ineligible for housing because you are a person from abroad, you have the right to ask it to review the decision. In addition, if your immigration status changes, you can reapply to the council at any time. There are now special arrangements for asylum seekers, who will be directed to accommodation in limited areas of the country.

If you are homeless

Local councils have a legal duty to help people who are homeless, or threatened with homelessness. This section describes the legal rights of homeless people.

People count as homeless if:

- they have no accommodation available for them to occupy, including any accommodation in another country
- they have a home but are in danger of violence or threats of violence, making it unreasonable for them to continue occupying it
- they are a family who are normally together, but are now living in separate homes because they have nowhere to live together
- their accommodation is moveable (for example a caravan or houseboat) and they have nowhere to place it
- they have accommodation but it is not reasonable to continue to occupy it.

People are considered as being threatened with homelessness if they are likely to become homeless within 28 days.

Who the council will help with accommodation

Not all people who are homeless, or threatened with homelessness, are provided with a home by the council. The council is, however, under a legal obligation to ensure that homeless people have somewhere to live if:

- they are 'eligible for assistance' (this excludes many people from abroad, see page 19)
- they are in 'priority need'
- they did not make themselves 'intentionally homeless'.

Who is in priority need?

The following groups of people are counted as being in priority need:

- people who live with dependent children aged either under 16, or under 19 if they are receiving full-time education or training
- all pregnant women, or someone who lives with a pregnant woman
- 16- and 17-year-olds, unless they have left care, (in which case social services are already responsible for ensuring they have accommodation) or social services owe them a duty to provide accommodation under childcare legislation
- 18- to 20-year-olds who were looked after, or accommodated by social services for any time when aged 16 or 17
- people who are homeless because of a fire, flood or a similar emergency
- people who are either vulnerable, or who live with someone who is vulnerable as a result of:
  - old age
  - mental illness
  - physical disability

– being in care

– having served in the armed forces

– having been in prison or custody

– becoming homeless because of violence or threats of violence
  that are likely to be carried out

– other special reasons.

In Wales, unlike England, people who are homeless as a result of
fleeing violence, leaving the armed forces or being released from
prison, do not also have to be vulnerable. Young people aged 18
to 20 at risk of sexual or financial exploitation (as well as people
formerly in care) are also considered to be in priority need in Wales.

The test of vulnerability is whether the homeless person would
be less able to fend for themselves than an ordinary homeless
person and more likely to suffer harm. Although councils
have discretion in deciding who is 'vulnerable', they must act
reasonably and unreasonable decisions have been successfully
challenged (see Challenging the council's decision on page 19).

Who is intentionally homeless?

If the council decides you are intentionally homeless, this means
it believes that you have given up accommodation you could
have continued to live in, or that it is your fault you have lost
accommodation (for example, by not paying the rent). Events
that happened some time in the past may be taken into account
if the council decides that these are the main cause of your
homelessness. However, councils must act reasonably and
take all facts into account. For example, if rent arrears were not
deliberate and arose because of circumstances beyond your
control, you should not be treated as intentionally homeless.
Councils' decisions can sometimes be successfully challenged
and overturned. If you are intentionally homeless the council
does not have to find you a long-term home, but if you are in
priority need, it is still under a duty to find you somewhere to
live temporarily and to give you advice and help with finding
your own accommodation.

If you have a home but are about to lose it, it is very important that you stay there for as long as you are entitled to. If you leave earlier, the council might decide you are intentionally homeless. In some circumstances this might mean waiting until you receive a court order to evict you. If you are in danger of homelessness always seek advice before leaving your home.

If you are not in priority need

If you are homeless but not in priority need, for example if you are a healthy person under retirement age without children, then the council does not have a legal duty to find you accommodation. It does, however, have a duty to provide you with advice and assistance. The council must first establish what your particular housing needs are and base its advice on those needs. In addition, the council has a power to provide you with accommodation if it is also satisfied that you are not homeless intentionally.

In practice this might not be much more than information on local hostels, cheap hotels and accommodation agencies; but some councils give more help than this and can offer a home even if you are not legally in priority need, so it is always worth applying to the council.

Where to go if you are homeless

If you are homeless or likely to be homeless in the near future, you should go to the Homeless Persons Section of the council. This will often be in the housing department. If you do not know where to find it, ask at the town hall or local council offices. When you arrive, make sure that you are seen by someone from the Homeless Persons Section. Some councils call it by a different name, for example, Homeless Families, Housing Emergency or Housing Welfare Section. You may be seen by someone from the Housing Aid or Advice Section first. Tell the person you see that you are homeless or about to become homeless. Make it clear that you need help urgently and have not come just to put your name on the housing list. Ask for the name of the person you see because you may need to speak to them again.

Do not be put off if the council is unhelpful. Remember you have a legal right to be given help and the council has a legal duty to provide it.

Which council to go to

Usually you should go to the council in the area where you become homeless or are about to become homeless. However, you have the right to apply to any council in the country. This is particularly important if you are homeless as a result of having to leave your home because of violence. You are entitled to apply to a council that is far away from your home. Long-term help for people in priority need will normally be given by a council with which they have a 'local connection'. Generally, you should be considered as having a local connection with a council if you, or anybody who normally lives with you:

- has lived in the council's area for six months out of the past year, or three years out of the past five
- has work (including voluntary work) in the area
- has close family who have lived in the area for at least five years
- has any other special connections with the area, for example you were brought up there.

But residence with, or employment by, the armed forces does not count as local connection, nor does residence in a prison, hospital or other institution if you have been staying in one of these.

If you apply to a council with which you (or anybody who lives with you) have any of these local connections then that council should be responsible for helping you.

If you have no local connection with the council to which you apply, that council must investigate your application and decide whether you are homeless, eligible for assistance, in priority need, and whether you are intentionally homeless. If it decides you have a right to help, but that you have no local connection with that council, then it can contact another council with which you do have a local connection, to make sure that it will help you. If you have a local connection with more than one council and you would prefer to live in a particular area, then your wishes should be taken into account, so it is important to make them clear. The council that you first apply to must make sure that the other council will help you; it must not simply send you along there. If you have nowhere to stay while these arrangements are being made, then the council that you first applied to must make sure that you have temporary accommodation.

If you have no local connection with any area, then the council to which you first apply has the duty to help you. People in fear of violence cannot be sent back to the area from which they have fled unless the council is satisfied that there is no risk of violence if they return to that area. The council should take account of your own fears of violence. If you think that it has not, seek advice.

The council's investigations

When you ask a council for help because you are homeless the council will check:

- whether you are homeless
- whether you are eligible for assistance
- whether you are in priority need
- whether you are homeless intentionally
- whether you have a 'local connection' with the area.

These investigations often involve detailed questions about your personal life. People who make false statements or withhold relevant information can be prosecuted and fined.

If you have nowhere to stay while the council is carrying out its inquiries and the council has reason to believe that you may be homeless, eligible for assistance, and in priority need, it must provide you with accommodation until it completes its inquiries and reaches a decision on your application. If the council decides that it does not have a duty to find you a home, it must provide you with its reasons in writing.

The kind of housing the council will provide

Councils may put homeless people initially into emergency or temporary accommodation. This can be a room in a bed and breakfast hotel, a hostel, a house waiting to be improved or demolished, or a home rented from a private landlord.

However, in England, councils should not use bed and breakfast accommodation for homeless people who are pregnant or have children, unless there is no other accommodation available. Even then, a council can keep you in bed and breakfast for no longer than six weeks. The Government announced that by 2010, 16- or 17- year-olds should no longer be placed in bed and breakfast hotels by local authorities, except in an emergency.

Sometimes, for example in a bed and breakfast hotel, you may not be able to take your furniture with you. If you cannot afford to store it and there is a risk of it being lost or damaged, the council must make sure it is stored in a safe place. It can make a reasonable charge for the temporary accommodation and for the furniture storage.

If, after completing its inquiries, the council is satisfied that you are homeless, eligible for assistance, in priority need, and not homeless intentionally, it must provide you with long-term accommodation (unless you have no local connection with it and have a local connection with another council, see above). This will usually, but not always, be a council house or flat. However, councils often offer their least popular types of homes to people who have been homeless and often make only one offer. You might be offered a housing association home (see page 27).

If you think the offer is unsuitable, you can ask the council to review it. If you turn down an offer of accommodation from the council, it might then decide that it has discharged its duty and does not have to offer any further help. You can, however, accept and ask the council to review the offer, so that you have somewhere to live if the review is unsuccessful.

Challenging the council's decision

If you do not agree with any decision made by the council, you have the right to ask it to review its decision. You must normally ask for the review within 21 days of being told about the decision. If the council does not change its decision it must give its reasons. The Housing Act 1996 imposes legal duties on local councils and gives homeless people legal rights. If you disagree with the council's decision, you might be able to challenge it in the county court if you believe the council has:

- misinterpreted the law
- reached an unreasonable decision
- not taken proper account of all the facts.

If you want to challenge the decision, it is essential to seek advice as soon as possible. A specialist advice agency should be able to help you challenge the council's decision and, as a last resort, may be able to advise you how to seek legal help to take the council to court.

People from abroad

Homeless people from abroad do not have any rights to help if they:

- are here in breach of the immigration laws
- were allowed into the country on the basis they would not claim any benefits
- fail the habitual residency test for welfare benefits
- are in breach of EU residency rules
- are asylum seekers who are excluded from claiming benefits.

Asylum seekers are covered by new arrangements (see page 12). People who might be excluded should seek advice, because they may still be entitled to some help with accommodation, food and other support.

Homeless young people

Young people aged under 18 have a right to help from the social services in addition to their rights under homelessness legislation. Social services have a duty to provide accommodation for any young person who is homeless and in need, and whose welfare is otherwise likely to be seriously prejudiced. A young person is counted as in need if they are unlikely to be able to achieve or maintain a reasonable standard of health or development without the provision of services by the council, or if their health or development is likely to be impaired, or if they have a disability. Social services will often meet this duty by asking the housing authority to help. Social services and housing departments should work closely together, but this may not always be the case.

Social services also have duties to provide accommodation and support for all 16- and 17-year-olds coming out of care. Social services also have a power (but not a duty) to provide accommodation for young people aged under 21 if that would promote or safeguard their welfare.

Other rights to rehousing

People who lose their homes as a result of action by the local council and through no fault of their own, will usually have a right to rehousing. There are a number of circumstances in which people can lose their homes because of council action. For example, the council might make a compulsory purchase order on the house and then demolish it, either because it is in bad condition or because it wants to use the land for other purposes. The council might decide the property has to be improved and this could mean that the tenants have to move out permanently. The right to rehousing does not apply, however, if the occupiers only have to move out temporarily. Anyone who is lawfully living in the property at the time the council starts its action is eligible for rehousing, so this right applies to owners and tenants. It does not apply to squatters or to people who move in after the council has started its action.

Although in practice people rehoused in these circumstances are usually offered some of the best types of housing, the council only needs to offer temporary accommodation at first and can expect people to wait for an offer of a permanent home.

People who do lose their homes in this way may also claim from the council:

- **A home loss payment**: for homeowners this is ten per cent of the market value of the property with a minimum payment of £4,400 and a maximum of £44,000. For tenants there is a flat-rate payment of £4,400. To qualify, the owner or tenant must normally have lived there for one year. The payment can be set off against rent arrears.

- **A disturbance payment**: to help with the costs of moving and setting up a new home. This covers the cost, for example, of removals, reconnections and adjusting curtains and carpets. In order to qualify, tenants must have been there at the time the landlord acquired an interest in the property, and must have been living there before the demolition or improvement programme was announced.

- **A well maintained payment**: if the property has been compulsorily purchased by the local council or has had a demolition or closing order on it, and if the property has been well maintained, an additional sum is payable to anyone who has undertaken that maintenance, including tenants.

Other council housing schemes

In addition to the schemes already described, councils often run special schemes for letting houses and flats. The most usual are:

- **Low-demand or hard-to-let schemes**: where the council has unpopular homes (for example, flats in older estates or tower blocks) that are often refused by other applicants, they may be offered to people on the housing register who would not normally have priority. So, for example, they may be offered to young single people and flat sharers.

- **Schemes for special groups**: some councils have a quota for particular groups, such as people recovering from a mental illness, ex-offenders or people sleeping rough.

There are many kinds of special schemes run by different councils, but the numbers of lettings involved are usually small. When you apply to the council for a home, ask for details of any schemes it runs.

Older people

Apart from letting ordinary homes to older people, local councils also make special provision for them. Most older people can lead fully independent lives, but some need extra help without needing the full care of a residential old people's home. For these people, local councils provide sheltered housing. Sheltered housing may be blocks of separate flats or small estates of bungalows. They are usually unfurnished, self-contained, and fitted with special features, for example an alarm to call a resident warden in emergencies. The privacy of the residents is preserved but social events may be organised for those who wish to participate. As with other types of council housing, there is, in many areas, a shortage of places in sheltered housing. Each council decides who should get priority. Many housing associations have similar schemes.

The council's offer of a home

The type and quality of council housing varies widely. Some types of property are much more popular than others. Many more people want to live in a house with a garden than in a tower block on a large estate. In many areas there is a severe shortage of the more popular types of homes and the council has to decide who should be offered the different types of property. Families with children are more likely to be offered houses with gardens or ground floor flats. Older people may also be offered ground floor or first floor flats. Fit people without children may only have the option of a high-rise flat.

Councils vary in the number of offers they are prepared to make; for example, some limit people from the housing list to three offers.

Some councils may ask you to state your preference when you first register with them, others may wait until they are in a position to make you an offer. It is important to discuss your preferences with the council and to make sure the officer you talk to understands the reasons for your particular preferences. You may, for example, need to live in a particular area for work or family reasons. But the more limited you are in the areas or types of property you are prepared to accept, the longer you are likely to have to wait. There may be certain areas or property types for which the council will refuse to consider you. It is generally difficult to get a council to bend these rules unless there is something very unusual about your circumstances – for example, strong medical reasons why you have to live in a ground floor flat.

It is also important to find out how many offers you will be made. If you are entitled to three offers, the second and third ones will not necessarily be any better than the first. You may be able to get an extra offer if you can show that the one made to you is grossly unsuitable or even a mistake; for example, if the council agreed to make you an offer in one area but then failed to do so. If you are thinking about refusing an offer, always discuss it fully with the housing officer and explain why you think it is unsuitable. The home you are offered may fall well short of what you hoped for, but if it is the usual type of property the council offers to people in your circumstances, there is likely to be little you can do in the short term to get a better property.

A growing number of councils operate choice-based lettings schemes, which means that homes are advertised and anyone who is interested can 'bid' for it. The bidder who has the highest priority on the list will be offered the property.

The council will normally give you a chance to look at the property before deciding. If it appears to be in bad condition, look closely to find out the reasons. If it needs redecoration the council may agree to do this before you move in, or may give you an allowance to do the redecorating yourself. If, however, there are more serious faults, you should ask the council to do the necessary repairs before you move in. If it refuses, seek advice from an independent agency (see Chapter 7). The council has legal obligations to carry out repairs (see page 142). An independent advice centre may be able to help you to get the council to make the repairs or to negotiate for an offer of another tenancy.

The council should also tell you how much the rent will be. This is usually payable weekly. On top of the rent, you also have to pay council tax for the provision of local council services such as refuse collection and schools. Many council tenants receive help with their rent and council tax payments through the housing benefit and council tax benefit schemes. See page 120 for details of these schemes.

Finally, the council should provide you with a written tenancy agreement and an explanation of it. This agreement sets out the rights and duties of both landlord and tenant. It should include details of the landlord's duties to carry out repairs. These agreements are normally in a standard form, so there is little or no scope for individuals to change any of the terms of the agreement. If there are things in it you do not like (for example, if you think the council is making you responsible for too many of the repairs), contact a local tenants' association or advice centre because you may, together with other tenants, be able to renegotiate the agreement or even challenge it in the courts.

Moving to another council house

If you are already a council tenant and want to move to another council property there are a number of ways of doing this.

Transfers

If you want to move within the area of your local council you can apply for a transfer. There are often many more people wishing to transfer than there are suitable properties available. Each council decides for itself who gets priority and some have very long lists of people wanting a transfer. The same rules apply to transfers as to applicants for housing (see page 9). If you have an urgent need to move (for example for serious medical reasons, or because you are overcrowded) you are more likely to get priority. Some councils also have arrangements for urgent transfers for people suffering from racial harassment. The council might also give you priority if there is a high demand for the type of property you are living in, for example, you want to transfer from a larger to a smaller home. However, if your present home is adequate but you want to transfer to one of the more popular properties, you may find it difficult or impossible to do so. The council should provide you with written details of how it decides who gets priority for transfers.

Exchanges

Tenants of social housing, including secure council and housing association tenants, have a legal right to exchange their home with other council or housing association tenants either within their own council's area, or in another area. You must get your landlord's permission to do this, but the landlord is only allowed to withhold permission for certain limited reasons and must in any event give you an answer within six weeks.

Your landlord, or the landlord of the person you want to exchange with, can only refuse to allow the exchange for one of the following reasons:

- your landlord has a court order to evict you
- your landlord has given a notice of proceedings for possession, or has started court proceedings giving one of the 'grounds for possession' numbered 1–6 on pages 93–94
- the accommodation you want to transfer to is substantially larger than you need
- the accommodation you want to transfer to is too small for your needs
- you or the other tenant has a job and accommodation in the grounds of a building not mainly used for housing purposes
- the landlord is a housing association or trust that only lets to certain groups of people in need and the proposed new tenant does not fit into one of these groups

- the landlord is a charity and the proposed new tenant is not the type of person who qualifies for help from that charity
- the accommodation is specially adapted for a person with physical disabilities and the proposed new tenant does not have disabilities
- the accommodation is one of a group of properties normally let to people with special needs, there are special facilities nearby for these people and the proposed new tenant does not need that type of special accommodation
- the accommodation is managed by a tenants' management co-operative and the proposed tenant is not willing to become a member of the co-operative
- you have been, or will be, taken to court for antisocial behaviour.

You are not allowed to give or receive any money as a part of the exchange. If you do, both you and the other tenant could be evicted (see page 25). Exchanges can be a useful way of moving areas, but they are rarely a way of getting better quality housing, because very few people are prepared to exchange their home for one of lower quality. There are a number of ways of finding another tenant to exchange with you:

- Ask your local council and the council for the area to which you want to move whether they keep lists of people wanting to exchange.
- There are a number of national exchange schemes, some free and some you have to pay for. You can find a list on the Directgov website under Home and Community, Exchanging council homes (see Useful contacts on page 194).
- Advertise in local papers in your own area and the area to which you want to move. You can also try advertising in local shop windows (especially newsagents) in the area to which you want to move.

Renting from a housing association

Housing associations and housing trusts are non-profit-making, independent organisations. They vary in size from associations that own one house, to those that have several thousand. Many receive money from the Government and from local councils, and are registered with the Housing Corporation, a government body that regulates them. They vary widely in the types of people they house. Some operate rather like local councils, catering for all types of people and giving priority to those with the most urgent need for housing. Others specialise in helping particular groups of people, for example older people, people with disabilities or those with other special needs.

Because they are non-profit-making, housing associations are usually cheaper and offer a better service than private landlords. However, rents can be higher than those charged by local councils. If the local council offers you the chance of a housing association home, it is worth checking what is available.

If you want to apply to rent a home from a housing association, you can find out from the local council which associations are operating in the area in which you want to live. Many associations take nominations from the local council, so you should ask your council whether it can nominate you. But the council can only nominate you if you have applied to its allocations scheme and you have been awarded sufficient priority. If the council cannot do so, contact the associations and ask them how you can apply. Each association has its own method of assessing applications and deciding who should be offered a home. Housing associations that are registered with the Housing Corporation are obliged by law to provide information on how they allocate their tenancies. Some will take applications directly, others will only take nominations through local agencies such as advice centres or social services. Ask the associations if any local agencies can nominate you. Each agency will have very few nominations, however, so they may not be able to help you. Many associations already have a backlog of applicants. Some keep waiting lists although they may close these to new applicants if they get too long. Others only accept applicants when they have a home ready to offer. Because they vary so widely, it is usually necessary to contact each association that you are interested in to find out how they operate and whether you have any chance of renting a home through them. In a few areas associations and the local council have set up common waiting lists, so you only have to apply once.

Moving to another housing association home

Housing association tenants have the same rights to transfers and exchanges as council tenants (see page 25). Contact your landlord for more details.

Renting from a private landlord

If you cannot afford to buy, do not qualify for a council or housing association home, or only want somewhere temporary, you may have to look for a private rented home. Some landlords will not take certain types of tenant; for example, they may not consider you if you are unemployed or if you have children. Some of the homes on offer may only be short-term lets known as shortholds, but landlords may be willing to renew the tenancy indefinitely.

Where to look

Many people find a home to rent through personal contacts, so it is worth asking friends, family and work colleagues if they know of any places. Landlords also advertise in shop windows and in daily and weekly newspapers and magazines. Tenants wishing to share with others also often advertise. Because of the shortage of places to rent in many areas, they are often let very quickly, so it is important to check newspapers and magazines as soon as they are published, telephone any suitable places immediately and be prepared to visit them the same day.

At the same time you can try accommodation agencies. These often advertise in the same places as landlords and are also listed in *Yellow Pages*. Most agencies make a charge, but they are only allowed to do so by law if you actually find and rent a home through them. It is illegal for an agency to make any charge if all they do is register your details or supply you with addresses of accommodation that you do not take up. Agencies are not allowed to ask you to pay a deposit that is returnable if no accommodation is found. Most agencies charge a fee of between one and two weeks' rent plus VAT.

An agency is allowed to charge for extra services provided, but only if this was done with your agreement or at your request. For example, an agency could charge if you ask it to negotiate on the tenancy agreement with your prospective landlord. This charge would be payable whether or not you finally get accommodation through the agency. Always ask what other charges might be involved when you first contact the agency. Agency charges vary widely. Some try to add on a range of charges just as you are about to sign an agreement, including fees for administration, for drawing up an inventory of furniture, or for carrying out a credit check on tenants. These extras can amount to several hundred pounds. You do not have to pay them and can try to negotiate, though you might, of course, lose the property.

If possible, use an agency that is a member of the the National Approved Letting Scheme (NALS), UK Association of Letting Agents (UKLAA), or belongs to the Association of Residential Letting Agents (ARLA), the Royal Institution of Chartered Surveyors (RICS), or the National Association of Estate Agents (NAEA) (see Useful contacts on pages 193–199). All of these have codes of conduct for their members, which should mean a better service from them and no extortionate fees. If you believe you should not have been charged or have been overcharged, get advice.

Some local councils run landlord accreditation schemes with which landlords who provide good standards can register. Check with your local council if they have a scheme.

Most agencies will want you to visit them to register. They will probably ask for details of your job and some will not register people who are unemployed. They may want references from your employer, bank, or a previous landlord. If they cannot offer you anything immediately, ring them at least once a day to ask if they have any places on their books. You can also try local estate agents and advice centres.

Negotiating the tenancy agreement

As landlords can sometimes pick and choose between a number of possible tenants, it may be difficult to try to bargain over the rent or the tenancy agreement. If you try to do so, you may risk losing the offer. However, these are the most important points to look out for:

- Carefully read any agreement you are asked to sign and if possible, get advice on it before signing.
- Check the type of letting that is being offered and how much security it gives you (see Chapter 2). Most places on offer are only short-term lettings, known as shortholds, but the landlord may be prepared to extend the tenancy when it runs out if you have been a reasonable tenant.
- Check what notice you have to give to end the tenancy. If you have a tenancy for a fixed term, check to see if you and the landlord can give notice to end the tenancy before the fixed term runs out.
- Check the rent. Does it include payments for gas, electricity and services, or are these extra?
- Check if there are any other extra charges.
- Check any obligations to repair and decorate the property. Some landlords try to pass these on to the tenants when they should in law be the landlord's responsibility.
- Check other obligations and rights of landlord and tenant that are written into the agreement.
- Check how much you have to pay in advance.

Typically, you may have to pay one month's rent in advance and a deposit of between one week's and two months' rent. In some areas there are schemes to help people who cannot afford a deposit. Ask a local advice agency if there are any schemes in your area. Since 6 April 2007 landlords and agents are now only allowed to take a deposit for an assured shorthold tenancy if it is safeguarded by a Tenancy Deposit Scheme. This should ensure that tenants will not have unfair deductions made from their deposits when they move out. If a landlord takes a deposit that is not protected by such a scheme, they will not be able to obtain an automatic possession order on assured shorthold tenancies (see page 65). Within 14 days, the landlord should give you information about which scheme is protecting your deposit. If s/he does not, you can to go to court to get the deposit paid into a scheme, or repaid along with compensation equal to three times the deposit. Schemes also have free Alternative Dispute Resolution services if you dispute any amount the landlord withholds at the end of your tenancy.

In addition to the tenancy agreement, you should also agree with the landlord a written list of the contents, the condition of the property, and any items provided with it, such as furniture or equipment. You will need to assess how far you feel you can negotiate with the landlord before signing an agreement. In areas of housing shortage where many tenants might be chasing one flat, you are obviously in a very weak bargaining position. Remember the tenancy agreement cannot take from you any of the rights given to you by law. Even if you have signed an agreement that says otherwise, you still have these rights. If the landlord suggests any changes in your tenancy agreement, always get advice before agreeing to them because they could seriously affect your rights.

Renting from a housing co-operative

Housing co-operatives are groups of people who collectively manage and usually own their own housing. They are democratically run so that everyone in the co-operative has an equal say in how it is managed. Some co-operatives are based in temporary short-life housing, others provide permanent homes.

Living in a co-operative means greater control for tenants over their own homes, but also a greater commitment of time and energy to managing your own housing. This often means doing unpaid work in your own time such as attending meetings, helping with administration, decorating, and repair work. Some of the larger co-operatives have elected committees and even employ people to do some of the work, but smaller co-operatives often expect all members to do their own share.

The members of the co-operative usually consist of the tenants and people waiting to become tenants. There are still only a few in existence and most of these are not open to new members. Your local housing advice centre, housing department or Citizens Advice Bureau should be able to tell you about any co-operatives operating in your area.

Buying a home

For many people, home-ownership offers the best opportunity of getting the home of their choice. But it generally involves higher costs in the early years, and problems can arise if you suffer a drop in income, perhaps through losing your job, relationship breakdown, or retirement, or when mortgage interest rates increase. It can then be difficult to keep up mortgage payments and to pay for repairs, so you need to feel sure about the security of your present level of income before deciding to buy.

Getting a mortgage loan

Most people who buy a home do so by taking out a loan for all or part of the cost. Interest is charged on the money loaned and repayments are made to the lender at monthly intervals, usually over a period of 20 to 25 years. The property is security for the money loaned, so that if the monthly repayments are not made, the lenders can take possession of the property and sell it to recover their money.

Before taking out a loan, it is always worth shopping around to find the best buy. The main sources of loans are banks and building societies, who can lend to any homebuyer. They differ in how much they are prepared to lend and also in the types of property on which they are willing to lend. For example, some lenders may be wary of lending on a flat on an upper floor where there is no lift in the block.

If they decide to offer you a loan, the lender will value the property you are planning to buy. The loan you will get is based on this valuation, not on the price you actually pay (although, of course, the two might be the same). Building societies often offer cheaper loans than banks and may be more helpful if you have problems repaying the mortgage. Some banks charge high rates of interest and may be more likely to evict you if you fall behind with mortgage repayments.

Mortgage brokers and financial advisers can also help to arrange a mortgage for you. However, be careful when approaching them, especially if they offer to find you a mortgage if you have been unable to get one directly from a building society or a bank. Mortgage brokers and advisers earn their living by charging commission or fees for arranging mortgages. This commission is earned in one of two ways. First, they can arrange an 'interest-only' mortgage and receive a commission from the company that arranges the investment. However, an interest-only mortgage may be more expensive and will probably be less advantageous for you (see page 36 for the pros and cons of interest-only mortgages). Second, the broker may arrange an ordinary building society or bank mortgage. However, you will have to pay the broker a fee for doing this.

A reliable broker should be registered with the British Insurance Brokers' Association (see page 193). If a broker is unable to arrange a mortgage for you, then any fee you have paid should be refunded. However, the broker is entitled to charge for any valuations of properties carried out on your behalf.

There are other sources of loans, but many of these should be approached with caution. You should always seek independent advice before agreeing to a loan from one of the sources listed below.

- Insurance companies can arrange endowment mortgages but usually only deal directly in loans for expensive properties at the upper end of the market.

- Your employer may be able to arrange a mortgage for you, either from their own funds, which can sometimes be at lower rates of interest, or through links with building societies or banks. However, if you get a loan at a low rate of interest, remember that if you leave that employer you will have to start paying a normal rate of interest, which could be difficult if you have borrowed a large amount.

- Builders of new homes may arrange special loans from a building society to help with the sale of the properties.

- Estate agents can often arrange a mortgage for customers, but check whether they are offering an interest-only or a standard repayment mortgage (see page 35).

- It is not advisable to borrow from a finance company in order to purchase a house. They tend to charge very high interest rates and are readier to evict people who fall behind with repayments. If you are thinking about borrowing from a finance company or small bank, get independent advice before signing any agreement. If you have already signed an agreement and are having second thoughts, get advice.

How much you can borrow

All lenders calculate how much they are prepared to lend on the basis of your income. The calculations are based on gross income, that is, before any deductions for tax. A proportion of guaranteed overtime payments or bonuses may also be taken into account. Different lenders use different methods of calculation to work out how much they will offer. For example, if there is a couple who are both working, a lender might take 3½ times the higher annual income plus the lower income.

So if a couple were earning £20,000 and £15,000 a year, they would take:

3½ x £20,000	=	£70,000
plus £15,000	=	£15,000
Total	=	£85,000

Under the Sex Discrimination Act 1975 it is illegal for lenders to discriminate against a woman by refusing to use her income as the higher one in their calculations if she is earning more than her partner. Lenders are also not allowed to discriminate against a single woman by offering her less than they would a single man earning the same amount (see page 53).

Some lenders offer very large loans in relation to your income. If you are offered such a loan think very carefully about whether you can afford it, not just now but also in the future if your income drops, or your expenses increase, or if mortgage interest rates go up. Many thousands of people have lost their homes because they could not afford the repayments. If in doubt, don't take out the loan.

Which type of mortgage to choose

There are two main types of mortgage repayment schemes and you will need to choose which suits you best.

- **Standard repayment mortgage**: this type of mortgage is available from building societies and banks. The monthly repayments are made up of the interest you pay on the amount borrowed and repayment of the loan itself (known as the capital). In the first year most of the monthly repayment consists of interest on the loan with only a small amount of capital paid off. But as each year goes by, you pay off more of the capital and the interest payments decrease. Repayments only change if the interest rate changes. It is also possible to get a fixed-rate mortgage, where the interest rate is fixed for an agreed period. The advantage of this is that you know what you will be paying and you could save money if interest rates go up, but equally you could end up paying more than you need if interest rates go down. Some lenders offer discounted mortgages. With these the monthly repayments start off lower than with standard repayments and then increase after a fixed period. You need to be sure you will be able to afford the full cost. On all these special offers you should look out for any catches, for example some lenders charge large fees for arranging the mortgage, some insist you take out expensive insurance or a mortgage guarantee through them. Some lenders require you to pay a large redemption fee, which can run to thousands of pounds, if you want to pay off a lump sum during the first few years of the mortgage.

- **Interest-only mortgages**: these are available through building societies, banks, insurance and investment companies. They are different from standard repayment mortgages because the capital borrowed is not repaid gradually each year, but is instead paid in a lump sum at the end of the mortgage term. In order to achieve this you take out an endowment policy with a life assurance company for which you pay monthly premiums, or another investment such as a pension or shares. The investment aims to pay off the lump sum at the end of the mortgage term.

With endowment mortgages, the whole loan is paid off by the insurance company if you die before the end of the term. However, many people have lost money on endowment and other interest-only mortgages because they are not guaranteed to pay off the full loan.

It is important to shop around for the best deal. The main questions you will want to ask in choosing the best type of mortgage are: Which is the cheapest? What if you have difficulty repaying the loan? What happens if you want to move? Interest-only mortgages may be less flexible if you want to move. If you run into difficulties in making the mortgage payments, then with an ordinary repayment mortgage it is often possible to extend the period of the loan and so reduce your monthly payments. This is not possible with interest-only mortgages. Recently, several companies offering endowment mortgages have raised repayments because projected returns would be too low to pay off the loan. Despite the fact that interest-only mortgages have disadvantages for most borrowers, some lenders try to persuade borrowers to opt for an interest-only mortgage because the lending agency gets a commission from the investment company. Standard repayment mortgages are the best buy for most people.

The Government has set standards for reasonable value mortgages with no hidden charges or terms, known as CAT standards. Non-CAT mortgages are not necessarily worse, but they are a good way of being sure your mortgage is a good buy. For more information, visit www.hm-treasury.gov.uk/documents/financial_services/mortgages

The cost of buying a home

Mortgage payments are not the only cost you will have to meet. There are a number of other expenses; some are one-off costs when you buy your home, others are recurring costs.

Initial one-off costs include:

- A fee for the valuation of the property that the lender carries out. The charges are usually on a sliding scale related to the price of the property. The average cost is around £180. Your own survey could cost £250 to £400, or more.
- You may need to make up the difference between what the lender will offer you as a mortgage and the price of the property. In addition, if the lender holds back some of the loan while repairs are done, you will need money to cover that. These sums could amount to several thousand pounds.
- If you employ your own solicitor to handle the legal aspects of the purchase you will have to pay fees that could be in the region of £300 to £600, or more.
- You will have to pay a fee to the lender's solicitor, probably in the region of £100.
- You may have to pay Land Registry fees. In most areas of the country all purchases have to be registered with the Land

Registry. The fees vary according to the purchase price of the property and whether it has previously been registered. As an example, on a £100,000 property that is already registered, the fee will be £100.

- Stamp duty is a tax payable on all properties costing more than £125,000. For most properties ranging from £125,001–£250,000, the duty payable is one per cent of the purchase price; three per cent between £250,001 and £500,000; and four per cent on properties costing £500,000 or more. The duty is paid on the whole purchase price and not just the amount above the cut off, for example, a house costing £180,000 would produce a stamp duty bill of £1,800. In areas designated by the Government as 'disadvantaged', properties up to £150,000 are exempt from stamp duty.

- Setting-up costs can include removal costs, connection fees for gas, electricity and telephone, and the cost of any new furniture, carpets, curtains and appliances.

Regular expenses include:

- If you buy a leasehold property (this will usually be a flat, see page 39) you will have to pay annual ground rent. A typical ground rent would be £50–£150 a year, but it could be higher.

- If you buy a flat in a block, you will usually have to pay service charges. Each occupier pays a share of the cost of common services such as cleaning and routine maintenance. Charges of £200 to £600 a year are not uncommon, but they could be higher if there are extensive services such as porters, lifts and gardens. Charges increase as the cost of providing the service rises. There is also usually an obligation to pay for your share of any major repairs such as replacing the roof or repairing the outside of the block.

- The lender will require you to have buildings insurance on the property against major damage such as fire. The amount you will have to insure is the cost of rebuilding the property, which can be higher than its market value. If you have a standard repayment mortgage it is also advisable to consider taking out a mortgage protection policy so that if you die the mortgage is paid off in full (endowment mortgages are automatically insured). In addition, it is advisable to insure the contents of your home. Some mortgage companies insist you buy insurance from them, which can be very expensive and cancel out savings from any special deals they are offering. Check before agreeing to the loan.

- Repairs do not occur at predictable intervals, but can be very expensive when they do come.
- Try to get details of fuel costs from the present owner.
- If your move means a longer journey to work you will have higher travel costs.

You should make at least an estimate of all these costs before committing yourself to buying.

Steps to buying a home

After shopping around for the best deal, you should contact the building society or bank where you are hoping to get a loan and ask for an agreement in principle that they will offer a mortgage and find out what their maximum loan to you would be. The next step is to decide what type of property to buy. You can get an idea of what is available in your price range from local newspapers and estate agents.

You may need to consider some of the following options:

- **Freehold, leasehold or commonhold**: most houses are freehold, almost all flats in the past have been leasehold, however a form of flat ownership called commonhold is becoming increasingly popular (see page 163). When you buy a freehold or commonhold property, you own it outright. When you buy a leasehold property you buy the right to occupy it for a fixed period. In practice, buying a leasehold property with a long lease (for example 99 years) is little different from buying a freehold, because you will probably sell while the lease still has many years to run. However, as the number of years remaining on the lease decreases, you may come across problems in getting a mortgage. For example many lenders are unlikely to lend on a lease with less than 50 years left to run. Even if you did manage to buy it, it could be very difficult to resell. If you live in a leasehold home you cannot normally be evicted when the lease runs out. If you live in a leasehold property you have rights to buy the freehold. (See page 162 for further details.)

- **Vacant or part possession**: if you buy your home with vacant possession, all previous occupants should move out when the purchase is completed. There should be a clause written into the contract of sale stating that vacant possession will be given, so that if the previous occupants do not move you can sue the person who is selling the property. You may find a relatively cheap home offered with 'part possession'. This means exactly what it says. You are entitled to possession of only part of the property and the rest is let to tenants. The tenants will almost certainly be protected from eviction and have as much legal right to live there as you. Their protection does not change because the property changes hands. The tenancy may not even end on the death of the tenant, because another member of the family living there may automatically inherit the tenancy. Most lenders will offer a mortgage only if you are buying with vacant possession. Therefore, even if you succeed in buying a property with tenants living in part of it, you could have difficulty reselling it in the future.

Finding a property

Estate agents in the area of your choice will have lists of available property displayed in their offices and will also send out lists by post free of charge. Estate agents do not charge buyers: it is the seller who pays them. Local newspapers also carry advertisements for properties. There are also many websites that offer homes for sale.

Negotiating the purchase

It may be possible to bargain on the price of the property, especially if demand is low and there is a shortage of prospective buyers. However, the reverse is true when demand is high and you may find you have been outbid by someone else. Ensure any written offer you submit states that it is made 'subject to survey and contract', which means that you are not bound to go through with it at this stage. Until you exchange contracts (see below) neither seller nor buyer is legally bound. If your offer is accepted you might be asked to pay a holding deposit. This could range from £50 to £250, possibly more, but it will be deducted from the final purchase price and you should get it back if the sale falls through. You can refuse to pay it, but if you decide to agree you should get a receipt for the deposit and make sure that it states that the estate agent or solicitor who is holding the deposit does so 'as stakeholder'.

Applying for a mortgage

As soon as you have agreed a price for the property you should apply for a mortgage. (See page 35 for details of the types of mortgages available.) You will have to fill in an application form and pay a fee for the valuation of the property. This valuation is undertaken for the lender by a qualified valuer and some lenders will let you see a copy of the report. It is important to realise that this valuation is not a detailed survey of the property and will not necessarily reveal, for example, structural defects that could be very expensive to put right.

It is therefore highly advisable to have your own independent structural survey done before going ahead with the purchase. This could cost up to, or more than £400 depending on the type of survey you have, but may save you thousands of pounds later on. It is often possible to save money by combining your lender's valuation survey with your own structural survey; ask your lender if you can do this. Most major lenders now offer a full survey at a competitive cost.

If the valuation report reveals that some repairs or improvements are necessary to the property, part of the loan may be withheld until these works are done satisfactorily. This is called a retention.

Because you cannot normally do the work before completing your purchase, you will need extra cash to make up the amount retained. The actual cost of the work may be higher than the amount of the retention, so make sure you can afford it by getting builders' estimates for the work.

In addition to checking on the property, the lenders will check your financial position. They will write to your employers to verify your income and possibly to your bank or landlord for a reference. If you are self-employed you will have to provide tax returns and accounts covering the past two or three years as proof of your income.

The legal steps

Most people use a solicitor to deal with the legal side of buying a home. This involves making inquiries to check whether anyone else has any claims to, or rights over, the property, whether services such as electricity, gas and water are connected, and whether there are any problems with the local council over planning permission. The process is known as conveyancing. You can also buy this service from private conveyancing companies.

It is possible to do the conveyancing yourself, although the seller's solicitor may be unhelpful if you do so. But if you are used to doing paperwork and do not feel intimidated by legal jargon or solicitors, you can save several hundred pounds. It is not nearly as complicated as many solicitors like to portray. This is particularly so for freehold properties. Leaseholds are more complicated and you would need to get legal advice over the lease.

If you decide to do it yourself there are guides available (see Useful publications on page 189). If, like most people, you decide to use a solicitor, there are a number of ways you can reduce costs:

- Ask your lender for a recommended solicitor. Your lenders will also use a solicitor to handle their legal work. Ask if you can both use the same solicitor because this will avoid duplicating work and may save costs.
- Ask friends for recommendations.

- Ask a number of solicitors for estimates of their costs. Find out whether these costs include VAT and 'disbursements' (ie costs paid on your behalf by the solicitor).

Once the final price has been agreed, you have a written offer of a mortgage and you or your solicitor have completed all the necessary investigations, you are in a position to exchange contracts. This means that you enter into a legally binding contract to buy the property on a certain date, so you must be sure that you have all the necessary money available and that the legal investigation has been properly completed. Your solicitor will send your signed contract together with a deposit (usually ten per cent of the purchase price) to the seller's solicitor and will receive a signed contract in return.

If you cannot afford the ten per cent deposit you may be able to negotiate a lower deposit of perhaps five per cent. If the seller does not agree, you will have to take out a short-term loan to cover it. If you have a bank account, ask to borrow from the bank. Try to avoid finance companies because their interest rates can be very high. Alternatively, it is possible to take out an insurance policy that will pay the vendor if you default on the contract. This can be cheaper than taking out a bridging loan. Ask your solicitor or lender for details.

Once you have exchanged contracts you are legally committed to buy, unless the property becomes unusable before the sale is completed. You should, however, check that the property is still insured by the seller up to the date of completion. The date when you complete the purchase is normally 28 days after the exchange of contracts, although this can be varied.

Home Information Packs

Anyone selling a property has to produce a Home Information Pack that will contain some of the necessary legal information listed above, along with a certificate on the energy efficiency of the property, which includes advice on how to cut carbon emissions and fuel bills (for more information, see Useful contacts on page 195).

Low-cost home-ownership schemes

There are a number of low-cost schemes to help people who might not otherwise be able to buy their own homes.

Shared-ownership schemes

These schemes are run by some local councils and housing associations. You take out a loan to buy a share in the value of the property (typically between 25 and 90 per cent) and pay rent on the remaining share. Under most schemes you have a legal right to buy out the remaining share held by your landlord, either in stages, or all at once.

Although these schemes are designed for people who cannot afford the full cost of ownership, they can sometimes work out more expensive than taking out a full loan on an older or smaller property. Check on property prices in the area to make sure there is nothing suitable in your price range. Even though you own only part of the property, you will normally have full responsibility for repairs and maintenance. You should check that you will be able to afford the cost of this. If you are interested in shared ownership you can get details from local councils and new town development corporations in the areas where you would like to live. You can get details of housing association schemes from the Housing Corporation (see Useful contacts on page 195).

Leasehold for older people

Some housing associations run special schemes to provide sheltered housing for older people. You pay 70 or 80 per cent of the cost of the property and the rest is made up by a government grant. When leaseholders leave, or die, they or their beneficiaries receive 70 or 80 per cent of the current market value of the property. Your local council should be able to give you the details of housing associations operating these schemes in your area.

HomeBuy

This scheme offers three ways of buying a home:

- **New Build HomeBuy**: shared-ownership schemes with housing associations, open to key workers (nurses, police officers, teachers etc), existing social tenants, and people in priority housing need.
- **Open Market HomeBuy**: you get a mortgage for 75 per cent of the value of your home, topped up by two other loans: one of 12.5 per cent from your mortgage lender, on which you pay no interest for five years, and a government loan of 12.5 per cent from the HomeBuy Agent on which you make no repayments at all, although it is repaid when you sell the property at a rate linked to the value of your home at that time. These schemes are open to existing tenants of social housing, people on a housing waiting list who are in housing need, key public sector workers in London, the South East and East of England, and some other priority first-time buyers.
- **Social HomeBuy**: tenants of social housing can buy the home they are living in either outright, or with shared ownership, at a discount.

Ask your local advice centre or council for details.

Cash Incentive Scheme

Local authorities can offer cash grants to tenants to buy a home in the private market. Ask your local council for details of any local scheme. It is up to your local authority whether they choose to run this scheme.

Information about Homebuy and the Cash Incentive Scheme can be found on the Communities and Local Government website www.communities.gov.uk

Other low-cost home-ownership schemes

Some local councils and housing associations have other schemes to offer lower-cost homes to people who could not otherwise afford to buy. For example, some buy and improve older properties and then resell them. Some also have arrangements with private developers to provide low-cost 'starter' homes for first-time buyers. Ask your local council and housing associations in your area.

Temporary and emergency housing

If you find yourself with nowhere to live and the council does not have a responsibility to provide you with housing, you may have to find short-term emergency accommodation (see page 12 for details of the help councils must give to homeless people). This section gives details of emergency and temporary housing. Some hostels take people in emergencies, others cater for longer-term stays. Bed and breakfast hotels are available if you can afford the prices. Some people, in desperation, resort to squatting. There are groups that provide short-life housing, but this is not usually available in an emergency.

Hostels

Hostels vary widely in the type and quality of accommodation they provide, in what they charge, in the types of people they are prepared to accept, and in how long they allow people to stay. They fall into three main groups:

- **Emergency hostels**: these are for people who are homeless and have nowhere to stay that night. They are sometimes called night shelters or direct access hostels. Some will take people without any money. Sometimes you are only allowed to stay for a short period, perhaps just for a few days. Anyone who moves into an emergency hostel should ask the staff for help with finding longer-term accommodation. Many have arrangements for residents to move on to longer-term hostels or permanent housing.

- **Longer-term hostels**: standards and prices vary enormously. Some are for particular groups, for example students or working women. Many will only take people of certain ages. Some provide meals, others have facilities to cook for yourself.

- **Supportive and therapeutic hostels**: these are for people with particular problems, who need some degree of support. Some are for temporary stays, for example hostels for people receiving treatment for addiction to drink or drugs, or for a psychiatric illness. Some provide long-term supportive homes, for example for people suffering from mental or physical disabilities.

For help with the cost of living in a hostel see page 120. To find a hostel in your area contact local advice agencies, the housing department, and the social services department of your local council.

Women's refuges

Women who have to leave home because of violence or threats of violence can try to get a place in a women's refuge. These provide shelter, advice and emotional support for women and their children, if they have any. You do not have to have any money and you will be helped to claim social security if you qualify. Because women's refuges do not like to turn people away, they can sometimes be crowded but they will always try to take you in an emergency and try to help you find somewhere to live in the longer term. You do not have to go to a refuge in the area in which you normally live. The organisation Refuge has an emergency 24-hour domestic violence freephone service (run in partnership between Women's Aid) if you need to find somewhere (see Useful contacts on pages 198–199).

Bed and breakfast hotels

Even the cheapest hotels can be more expensive than many hostels and they often have very poor standards. You will usually have to pay in advance and may have to share a room if you cannot afford very much. You may be able to get help to pay some or all of the cost (see page 120). For details of cheap bed and breakfast hotels in your area contact local advice agencies.

Squatting

Some homeless people are forced to squat because they cannot find anywhere else to live. Squatters are people who enter into, and stay in property without the permission of the owner. They can be evicted very rapidly (see page 102), but squatting itself is not a crime. However, you risk committing an offence if you break into a property to squat and damage the doors or windows. You may also commit an offence if you fail to leave when legally ordered to do so.

Some squatters are able to stay for several months, others are evicted after a few weeks or even days. In some circumstances you might have to leave within 24 hours, or even as soon as you are asked to do so (see page 103). You should look at all other ways of solving your housing problem before deciding to squat.

If you decide that squatting is your only option, there are a few basic rules to observe in order to avoid breaking the law:

- If bailiffs come with a warrant to evict you, do not obstruct them or refuse to leave.

- Do not break in if you can avoid it. You could be charged with committing criminal damage. If you do break anything, mend it as soon as possible.

- Never squat at a property that looks as if it might be lived in.

- Try to find a place that has been empty for some time.

- Do not use the gas or electricity supplies without making proper arrangements with the appropriate fuel company. If you do so, you could be charged with theft.

If you are thinking about squatting, it is much better to do it through an organised group than on your own. For advice and details of local groups contact the Advisory Service for Squatters (see Useful contacts on page 193) and read the Squatters' Handbook (see Useful publications on page 190).

Short-life housing

The idea of short-life housing is to make use of houses that are waiting to be repaired, improved, or demolished rather than leaving them standing empty. The properties that are used in this way are usually owned by local councils or housing associations. Most commonly, a group of people take over the houses for a limited period and patch them up to make them habitable. The period varies – it can be as short as a few months, or as long as five or more years. In most cases the occupiers do not have security and have to leave when the landlord wants the property back. There is often no guarantee of alternative housing at the end of the period.

Most short-life housing groups only take people without children. Many are organised as tenants' co-operatives (see page 31). You will be expected to play a full part in running the group, going to meetings, and helping with repair work. There is usually a waiting list for housing and many do not take new members. For details of local short-life groups contact your local advice agency.

Discrimination: race, sex, disability, faith and sexual orientation

Racial discrimination

Black and other ethnic minority people often suffer from discrimination in their search for a home. There is evidence of discrimination by some private landlords, accommodation agencies and estate agents, which is against the law. This section describes the law as set out in the Race Relations Act 1976 and tells you what to do if you encounter illegal discrimination.

What is discrimination?

The Race Relations Act defines three types of discrimination:

- Direct discrimination means treating someone less favourably than others because of their race.
- Indirect discrimination means applying a rule that cannot be justified on non-racial grounds and which, whether intentionally or not, has a disproportionately adverse effect on a particular racial group. So, for example, it would be indirect discrimination for a landlord to say that s/he would not take any tenant who cooked curry.

- Victimisation means treating one person less favourably than another because s/he has made a complaint, or given information about alleged illegal racial discrimination.

Discrimination by accommodation agencies and landlords

It is illegal for accommodation agencies to discriminate either directly, or indirectly, against anyone seeking accommodation by:

- refusing or deliberately omitting to provide details of available accommodation
- refusing or deliberately omitting to provide their services on the same terms, in the same manner, and of the same quality as would normally be provided to other people.

So, for example, even if a landlord tells an accommodation agency that s/he does not want any black tenants, it is still illegal for the agency to follow this instruction and to exclude black applicants. However, small premises are exempt from this provision (see below).

It is illegal for landlords, both private and public, or anyone acting on behalf of a landlord, to discriminate on racial grounds either directly or indirectly by:

- offering the accommodation on inferior terms
- refusing an application for a tenancy
- treating the applicant in any way less favourably than other people in need of such accommodation.

It is also illegal for landlords or tenants to discriminate in the subletting or assigning of tenancies, for example, a landlord cannot refuse to allow a tenant to sublet to a particular person on the grounds of that person's race.

Small premises

Small premises are exempt from the forementioned provisions. It is not illegal for a landlord or an accommodation agency to discriminate on racial grounds by the letting of accommodation that counts as small premises. In order to count as small premises all of the following must apply:

- the landlord or a near relative (defined as a wife, husband, partner, parent, child, grandparent, grandchild, brother or sister) must live on the premises and intend to continue living there

- the landlord or near relative must share some of the premises with the tenant – this covers bathrooms, kitchens and living rooms, but not means of access or storage space

- there is, in addition to the accommodation occupied by the landlord or near relative, accommodation for no more than two other separate households if the property is divided into separate lettings, or for no more than six other people in the case of a boarding house.

Discrimination against existing tenants

It is illegal for a landlord or anyone managingaccommodation to:

- refuse or deliberately omit to give normal benefits and facilities to anyone occupying the premises because of their racial origin

- evict someone or subject them to inferior treatment because of their racial origin.

This applies to all occupiers even if the accommodation falls within the definition of small premises (see above).

Inducing or helping others to discriminate

It is illegal for a landlord to instruct an accommodation agency or an employee to discriminate on racial grounds. This would include, for example, expressing a 'preference' for tenants of a particular racial group because this is, in effect, treating one group more favourably than another. If a landlord tells an agency that accommodation is exempt from the law because it qualifies as small premises, the agency is not permitted to accept the landlord's word, but must take all reasonable steps to check that it does meet all the conditions required to qualify as small premises.

In addition to these specific provisions, the Race Relations Act also places a duty on local authorities to make appropriate arrangements to ensure that their various functions are carried out with due regard to the elimination of unlawful racial discrimination, and to the promotion of equality of opportunity and good relations between people of different racial groups.

Estate agents

Estate agents are in the same position as accommodation agencies. It is illegal for them to discriminate against anyone seeking their services by:

- refusing or deliberately omitting to provide their services
- refusing or deliberately omitting to provide services on the same terms, in the same manner, and of the same quality as would normally be provided to other people.

So, for example, it is illegal for an estate agency to accept an instruction from someone wanting to sell their house that they would not consider a black buyer. However, it is not illegal for someone who is the owner of a property to discriminate if they sell it privately without advertising or using an estate agent.

Action against racial discrimination

Anyone who suffers from illegal racial discrimination by accommodation agencies, landlords, or estate agents, can take proceedings in the county court. They can get a declaration of their rights, damages (including damages for injury to feelings) and an injunction or order against the person or agency that has discriminated. Advice and assistance are available from the Equality and Human Rights Commission, which also has the power to conduct a formal investigation into organisations in order to eliminate discrimination. The Commission has issued a Code of Practice for the elimination of racial discrimination in housing (see Useful contacts on page 194).

Sex discrimination

The Sex Discrimination Act 1975 makes many forms of discrimination against women or men, on the grounds of their sex, illegal. The provisions against discrimination over housing are very similar to those of the Race Relations Act. The Sex Discrimination Act covers:

- direct discrimination, meaning treating a woman less favourably than a man because she is a woman, or vice versa
- indirect discrimination, meaning applying a rule that has a disproportionately adverse effect on men/women
- victimisation, meaning treating a man/woman less favourably because s/he has tried to enforce his/her rights under the Sex Discrimination Act.

As with racial discrimination (see above) it is illegal to discriminate against men/women in the sale or letting of property, and in the treatment of people occupying accommodation. So, for example, it is illegal:

- for local councils to treat female applicants for housing less favourably than male applicants, or vice versa
- for estate agents and accommodation agencies to discriminate against men/women
- for landlords to offer female tenants worse facilities than male tenants, or vice versa.

Small premises are, however exempt, as they are under the Race Relations Act (see page 50).

When applying for a mortgage it is illegal for the building society or bank to treat a female applicant less favourably than a male applicant, or vice versa.

Disability discrimination

The Disability Discrimination Act makes it unlawful to discriminate against someone with a disability in:

- access to goods, facilities and services
- the management, buying and renting of property.

Discrimination occurs where a person with disabilities is treated less favourably than someone else, and the treatment is for a reason relating to the person's disability and cannot be justified. Most resident landlords are exempt. Discrimination can also occur where there is a failure to make a reasonable adjustment for a disabled person, or where the landlord unreasonably withholds consent to improvements.

Sexual orientation discrimination

Under the Equality Act (Sexual Orientation) Regulations 2007 providers of goods, facilities and services must ensure they are not treating their customers unfairly on the grounds of sexual orientation. Most resident landlords are exempt.

Faith discrimination

Under the Equality Act 2006 it is illegal to for landlords, their mangers, or sellers of properties to discriminate against anyone on the grounds of their religious belief or lack of belief. Most resident landlords are exempt.

Action on discrimination

For advice and help on discrimination contact the Equality and Human Rights Commission (see Useful contacts on page 194).

Keeping your home

2

Introduction

People can be in danger of losing their homes for a number of reasons. The degree of protection you have from eviction depends on whether you own or rent your home and, if you rent it, what type of tenant you are. This chapter explains how much protection, or security of tenure, you have. If you are in danger of losing your home, you should always get expert advice.

Private tenants and licensees

All people who rent from a private landlord have some degree of protection from eviction. But the amount of protection you have varies enormously depending on the arrangements you have made with the landlord, and the date the tenancy began. The law relating to protection from eviction is very complex. The degree of protection you have depends in part on when your tenancy started. Page 67 deal with tenancies that began before 15 January 1989. Page 58 deal with tenancies that began on or after 15 January 1989.

In very broad terms, people renting from private landlords fall into one of the following categories:

- The majority of new lettings are known as assured shorthold tenancies. These are short-term tenancies of six months, although landlords are often willing to let tenants stay for longer.

- Most tenants have non-resident landlords (that is landlords who do not live in the same house). These tenants are generally fully protected if their tenancy began before

15 January 1989 and it is very difficult for the landlord to evict them as long as they pay the rent and act reasonably. If their tenancy began on or after 15 January 1989, they will usually be assured shorthold tenants, with less protection.

- The next largest group is tenants of resident landlords (that is landlords who live in the same house). In general these tenants have very limited protection. The landlord has a right to evict them but the tenant may be able to delay the eviction for a while if they do not share living accommodation with the landlord.

- There is a smaller group of people renting their homes who have very little security. They may have a holiday let, or a licence, or a company let. With these you have very little or no protection from eviction.

- People who share their home, such as flat sharers. Their position is very complicated and depends on the arrangements made with the landlord. Some are fully protected, others have very little protection.

- People who live in tied housing whose home is provided with the job. Generally they have only limited protection.

- Some agricultural workers have special protection and also special rights to rehousing if they are evicted.

This section is designed to help you decide what kind of letting, and what degree of protection, you have. It gives only an outline of the law. If you are at all unclear about your own position you will need to get expert advice. Advisers can find more legal details in the guides listed in Useful publications on page 189.

Tenant or licensee?

The first question to answer is whether you are a tenant at all. Just because you make regular payments to the owner of your home you are not automatically a tenant in the eyes of the law. The majority of people who rent their home are tenants, but a few people in these circumstances are in fact only licensees. It is essential to find out whether you are a tenant or a licensee, because many of the rights given by law apply only to tenants and not to licensees. Unfortunately, although the distinction between the two is very important, in practice the dividing line between them can be unclear and borderline cases can only be decided by looking at individual circumstances. The difference between them is not defined in any legislation.

In broad terms a tenant is someone who has a legally binding right to occupy a property and to exclude other people from it. A licensee is someone who merely has the permission of the owner to be in the property. So, for example, at one extreme someone who visits your house as a guest is your licensee. People living in hostels or staying temporarily in a hotel are usually licensees. On the other hand, someone who pays rent on a house or flat for their sole occupation is usually a tenant.

In deciding whether you are a tenant or a licensee the first question is: is there a written agreement? Contracts between landlords and tenants or licensees do not have to be in writing. But if there is a written agreement this is the first place to look. Does it mention 'tenant' or 'tenancy', 'licensee' or 'licence'? However, you are not necessarily a licensee just because your landlord has made you sign a piece of paper that describes you as one. If the matter goes to court, the judge should look at all the circumstances surrounding the agreement to make sure it is not merely a sham. The points the court will consider are:

- Does the occupier have 'exclusive possession' of the accommodation? This means that the occupier has the exclusive right to live in the premises. Unless you have this right over at least part of the accommodation you cannot be a tenant. One pointer here is whether the accommodation has its own locked door with keys held only by the occupier. If you are forced to share all the accommodation with other people you may well be a licensee. Where people are sharing voluntarily (as with flat sharers) the position is even less clear (see page 82 for further details).

- What were the true intentions of the landlord and occupier when they came to their agreement? It is almost certainly a tenancy if there is a letting of self-contained accommodation and you pay rent. If, however, you are in a hotel or hostel and the owner has unrestricted access to your accommodation you will be a licensee. If the accommodation is provided as an act of friendship or free of charge, you are also likely to be a licensee.

If your landlord claims that you are a licensee but you believe that in reality you are a tenant, you can dispute this claim and, if you win, gain all the rights of a tenant. If you have your own self-contained accommodation and are not a lodger, then you are probably a tenant, regardless of any agreement you might have signed.

The following sections are for tenants. If you are a licensee, turn to page 56. If your tenancy began before 15 January 1989 turn to page 67.

Tenancies that began on or after 15 January 1989

The Housing Act 1988 introduced two new types of lettings: assured and assured shorthold tenancies. Most tenancies that began before 15 January 1989 are not affected and keep the same legal protection. After that date there are no new protected tenancies (or secure housing association tenancies) unless:

- the tenancy was agreed before that date
- the tenant was previously the fully protected tenant (see page 67), or secure housing association tenant (see page 90) of the same landlord
- the new tenancy is being granted as suitable alternative accommodation as part of a possession order and the court has directed that a protected tenancy (or secure housing association tenancy) is granted.

Pages 58–66 give details of assured and assured shorthold tenancies.

Assured Tenancies: tenancies excluded from protection

After 15 January 1989 all lettings by private landlords and housing associations are assured tenancies or assured shorthold tenancies unless they are one of the following types of tenancy:

- Protected tenancies (see page 67), secure housing association tenancies (see page 90), and tenancies protected by the Rent (Agriculture) Act 1976 (see page 78), as long as these tenancies started before 15 January 1989.

- Housing association tenancies that were granted as temporary housing to people accepted as homeless by a local council.

- Tenancies that were entered into or agreed before 15 January 1989.

- Homes where the rateable value or rent is very high: if the rateable value was above £1,500 in Greater London or above £750 elsewhere on 31 March 1990. There are very few properties with rateable values above these limits. If the tenancy began on or after 1 April 1990 and the rent is more than £25,000 a year, then it is not an assured tenancy.

- Tenancies where the rent is very low: where no rent is paid, or the rent is less than two-thirds of the rateable value if the tenancy began before 1 April 1990 or, after that date, if the rent is less than £1,000 a year in London or £250 a year elsewhere. Payments for rates, services, maintenance and insurance are not included in calculating the rent. Again, this affects a very small number of tenancies.

- Business tenancies to which Part II of the Landlord and Tenant Act 1954 applies.

- Licensed premises – tenancies of dwellings licensed for the sale of alcohol on the premises.

- Agricultural land – tenancies let with more than two acres of agricultural land and holdings occupied by the person responsible for farming the land.

- Lettings to students by educational institutions.

- Holiday lettings – a tenancy is not protected if the purpose of the letting is that the tenant occupies it for a holiday. However, a tenancy is not necessarily a holiday let just because you have signed a piece of paper describing it as that. If the tenant argues that this is a sham, the courts must look at the true circumstances of the letting. If there is a written agreement stating it is a holiday let, then the burden is on you to prove that neither you nor the landlord intended to create a holiday let. One way to do this would be to prove that the landlord knew you were not on holiday.

- Resident landlords – to qualify as resident the landlord must have lived in the same building as the tenant, continuously since the start of the tenancy. The landlord does not count as resident however, if s/he and the tenant live in separate flats in a purpose-built block of flats.

- Crown tenancies – the landlord is the Crown or a government department.

- Public sector tenancies – tenants of local councils, new towns, housing co-operatives and other public housing bodies. However, housing association tenancies can be assured tenancies (see page 58).

All assured tenancies created on or after 28 February 1997 will be assured shorthold tenancies unless the landlord has served a notice on the tenant that it is not a shorthold, or the tenant previously had a different kind if tenancy with that landlord. These are now the most common type of new tenancy. For more details of assured shorthold tenancies see page 65.

Assured tenants: protection from eviction

Assured tenants can only be evicted by a court order. They do not have to leave just because the landlord tells them to, or because the tenancy agreement has run out. Anyone whose landlord asks them to leave should get advice immediately.

If the original tenancy was for a fixed term only, for example six months or a year, and when that time runs out the landlord does not offer you a new tenancy of the same premises, then the assured tenancy automatically becomes a periodic tenancy, which means that it continues indefinitely and the landlord can only evict you by going to court and proving one of the grounds for eviction set out below.

Notice of proceedings for possession

Where the landlord wants to seek a possession order against an assured tenant, s/he must first give the tenant a notice of proceedings for possession in the proper legal form. The notice must specify which of the grounds for possession (set out below) the landlord is seeking to prove, and why the landlord thinks the particular ground applies to the tenant; for example, details of the level of rent arrears. The length of notice that must be given depends on which of the grounds for possession the landlord specifies.

Normally, the landlord cannot go to court unless a proper Notice of Seeking Possession has been served on the tenant. However, if it considers it just and equitable to do so, the court can decide to waive this rule in any case except one where the landlord is seeking possession on Ground 8 below.

Grounds for possession

The landlord can try to persuade the court that s/he should get a possession order on any of the grounds listed below.

For each ground, a number of different conditions apply. These numbered conditions are detailed on pages 64–65 and shown in italics after each ground for possession.

For Grounds 1–8, the court must grant possession if the case is proved.

Ground 1 Before the start of the tenancy the landlord had at some time occupied the accommodation as his/her only or principal home, or the property is required as the only or principal home for the landlord and his/her spouse or civil partner and the landlord did not buy the property with the tenants already living there. (*Conditions 1, 7, 9, 10*)

Ground 2 A mortgage lender requires vacant possession of the property to sell it. (*Conditions 1, 6, 7, 9, 10*)

Ground 3 The property was let for a fixed-term of not more than eight months and it had been occupied as a holiday letting within the previous 12 months (see page 60 for the definition of a holiday letting). (*Conditions 2, 7, 9*)

Ground 4 The tenancy was for a fixed-term of no more than 12 months and it had been occupied as a student letting within the preceding 12 months. (*Conditions 2, 7, 9*)

Ground 5 The accommodation has been let temporarily but is now required for letting to a minister of religion. (*Conditions 1, 7, 9*)

Ground 6 The landlord intends to demolish, reconstruct or carry out substantial work on the property and all of the five conditions are fulfilled. Firstly, that the tenant is not willing to allow the landlord to gain access to do the works, or it would be impracticable to gain the necessary access. Secondly, that the tenant is not willing to move into only part of the accommodation to allow the work to be carried out, or it would be impractical for the tenant to do so. Thirdly, that the landlord cannot reasonably carry out the work without gaining possession of the property. Fourthly, that the landlord did not buy the property with the tenant already living there. Fifthly, that the assured tenancy did not come into being as a result of the present tenant gaining the right to succeed to a previous fully protected tenant who had died. (*Conditions 1, 7*)

Ground 7 The tenant inherited the tenancy under the will or intestacy of the previous tenant and the landlord has begun possession proceedings no later than 12 months after the death of the former tenant, or from the date at which the court decides the landlord became aware of the death. (*Conditions 1, 7*)

Ground 8 There are at least eight weeks' rent arrears both when the notice of proceedings for possession is served on the tenant, and at the date of the court hearing. (*Conditions 2, 4, 6, 7*)

For the second set of grounds for possession (Grounds 9-17), the court may grant a possession order, but only if the landlord can prove the case and the court thinks that it is reasonable to grant an order. The court also has the power to suspend any possession order either for a fixed period, or indefinitely, subject to certain conditions. For example, the court might make an order for possession under Ground 10 because of rent arrears but suspend the order to give the tenant an opportunity to pay off the arrears. Then, as long as the tenant pays off the agreed amounts, the order will not take effect.

Ground 9 Suitable alternative accommodation is available for the tenant. In deciding whether the alternative accommodation is suitable the court must take into account the degree of protection from eviction it offers, the rent charged, the type and size of property offered, and its distance from the tenant's place of work. This does not mean, however, that the alternative accommodation has to be of the same standard as the present home. (*Conditions 1, 8*)

Ground 10 There are rent arrears both when the notice of proceedings for possession is served on the tenant, and when the possession proceedings begin. (*Conditions 2, 6, 8*)

Ground 11 The tenant has persistently delayed paying the rent, whether or not there are outstanding arrears when the possession proceedings are begun. (*Conditions 2, 6, 8*)

Ground 12 The tenant has broken one of the terms of the tenancy agreement. (*Conditions 2, 6, 8*)

Ground 13 The tenant, or someone else living in their home, has damaged or neglected the property. (*Conditions 2, 6, 8*)

Ground 14 The tenant, or someone else living in, or visiting their home, has caused a nuisance or annoyance to neighbours or other people visiting the area, or has been convicted of using the property for illegal or immoral purposes, or committed an offence in the neighbourhood. (*Conditions 3, 6, 8*)

Ground 14A The tenants are a married couple or living together as husband and wife or are civil partners and one has left because of violence or threats of violence against him/her or a member of the family, and s/he is unlikely to return. Only registered social landlords and charitable housing trusts can use this ground – it cannot be used by ordinary private landlords. (*Conditions 2, 6, 8*)

Ground 15 The tenant, or someone else living in their home, has damaged furniture provided by the landlord. (*Conditions 2, 6, 8*)

Ground 16 The property was let in consequence of the tenant's employment by the landlord, or a previous landlord of the property, and the tenant is no longer in that employment. (*Conditions 1, 8*)

Ground 17 The tenant aquired the tenancy by knowingly or recklessly making false statements to the landlord. (*Conditions 2, 8*)

Conditions on grounds for possession
The following conditions apply to some grounds for possession for assured tenancies. Those that apply are shown above in italics after each of the numbered grounds.

1 The landlord must give at least two months' notice.

2 The landlord must give at least two weeks' notice.

3 The landlord can start proceedings as soon as notice is served.

4 The landlord cannot go to court under any circumstances unless proper notice has been served.

5 If the tenancy is for a fixed term, the landlord cannot go to court until the fixed term has expired.

6 If the tenancy is for a fixed term, the landlord can go to court before the end of the fixed term if the tenancy agreement states that the tenancy can be ended for the reason given in the ground for possession.

7 The court must order possession if the ground is proved.

8 The court may decide not to grant possession if it is not reasonable to do so, and may suspend any possession order, subject to conditions being fulfilled, such as payment of arrears.

9 The landlord must have served notice on the tenant before the tenancy began in order that possession might be sought on these grounds.

10 The court can waive condition 9 above, if it is just and equitable to do so.

Assured shorthold tenancies

Assured shorthold tenancies are tenancies that began on or after 15 January 1989. Most new tenancies are assured shortholds. If you have a shorthold tenancy that began before that date, see page 75.

Assured shorthold tenancies are similar to other assured tenancies (see page 58), except that the landlord, without having to prove any other grounds for the order, is entitled to get a court order to evict the shorthold tenant once the agreed period of the tenancy has come to an end. The landlord must however allow at least six months from the beginning of the tenancy.

If the tenancy began before 28 February 1997, the landlord must follow the proper legal procedures to do this. The procedures are:

- the landlord must give the tenant at least two months' notice in the correct legal form and at the right time that s/he requires possession of the property
- the tenancy must be for a period of at least six months
- the landlord must get a court order
- before the tenancy begins, the landlord must have served a notice on the tenant in exactly the form laid down in law. The notice informs the tenant that the tenancy is a shorthold.

If the tenancy began on or after 28 February 1997, it will automatically be an assured shorthold unless:

- the tenant succeeded to a tenancy or it has been assigned to them
- it was previously a secure tenancy (see page 90)
- it was previously an ordinary assured tenancy and the tenant has not served a legal notice on the landlord that it will be a shorthold tenancy
- the landlord has notified the tenant that the tenancy is to be a fully assured tenancy
- the tenancy arose at the end of a long lease; these are normally found in owner-occupied flats
- it is one of a certain type of assured agricultural occupancy (see page 78).

For assured shorthold tenancies that began on or after 28 February 1997, the landlord must give the tenant two months' notice to end the tenancy, and the court cannot order the tenant to leave until at least six months from the start of the tenancy. Before that time, shorthold tenants can be evicted for the same reasons as ordinary assured tenants (see the previous section).

Tenants with resident landlords

The protection from eviction of tenants of resident landlords will depend on whether or not they share living accommodation with the owner, or their family, in their only, or principal home.

If you share such living accommodation, you are an 'excluded occupier'. The landlord has to give a Notice to Quit, which does not have to be in writing and after it expires, s/he can evict you without even needing a court order.

If the landlord is resident in the building (see page 68 for what is meant by resident) but the tenant does not share any such living accommodation with the landlord or his or her family, then the tenant has basic protection. (See page 81 for more information.)

Assured agricultural occupancies

Agricultural workers who live in tied housing and whose occupancy began on or after 15 January 1989 have special protection under the Housing Act 1988. The type of protection and those covered by it are broadly the same as the provisions of the Rent (Agriculture) Act 1976. For details see page 78, except that references to the Rent Act are now the Housing Act 1988 and the list of grounds for possession will now be replaced by Grounds 1–15 and 17 listed on pages 61–64. Ground 16 does not apply to assured agricultural occupiers.

Tenancies that began before 15 January 1989

The Rent Act 1977 gives varying degrees of protection to most tenancies that began before 15 January 1989. Those that have full protection are known as regulated tenancies. They are also referred to in this guide as protected tenancies. But some are excluded from full protection.

Tenancies that began before 15 January 1989 but that are not fully protected by the Rent Act 1977

The following types of tenancies are exempt from full Rent Act protection:

- Homes where the rateable value is very high – this usually means where the rateable value was above £1,500 in Greater London or £750 elsewhere on 31 March 1990. However, some with higher rateable values may still be protected. In practice only a tiny number of lettings are excluded from protection because they are above these limits.
- Certain shared-ownership leases.
- Tenancies where the rent is very low – again this affects only a very small number of tenancies, but tenants may not be protected if they do not pay any rent or if the annual rent is less than two-thirds of the rateable value on 31 March 1990.
- Dwellings let with other land where the tenancy of the dwelling itself is not the main purpose of the letting.

- Tenancies where the rent includes payment for board. 'Board' means the provision of meals, not just a drink. Some landlords tried to exclude their tenants from Rent Act protection by providing very limited board. A box of groceries provided every week should not count as board, but a continental breakfast prepared and served on the premises probably would. If the landlord claims you are not a protected tenant because you receive board, you should get advice.

- Tenancies where the rent includes payment for a substantial amount of 'attendances'. Attendances mean personal services to the tenant, for example, cleaning the tenant's room, but do not include the cleaning of common parts of the building or the provision of gas, electricity, or hot water. If the value of the attendances provided is substantial (the definition is the same as for substantial board – see above) then the tenant only has basic protection. If the value of the attendances does not form a substantial part of the rent, then they do not affect the tenant's security and the tenant remains fully protected.

- Lettings to students by educational institutions.

- Holiday lettings – see page 60 for the definition of a holiday letting.

- Agricultural holdings – these are not protected. However, many agricultural workers in tied housing are protected by the Rent (Agriculture) Act 1976, see page 78.

- Licensed premises.

- Resident landlords – the most important exemptions from full Rent Act protection are lettings by resident landlords. To qualify as resident, the landlord must have lived in the same building as the tenant continuously since the start of the tenancy. The landlord does not count as resident, however, if the building is a purpose-built block of flats, unless the landlord lives in the same flat as the tenant.

However, lettings by resident landlords of unfurnished accommodation that began before 14 August 1974 are fully protected (unless they are exempt on some other grounds, for example, sharing living accommodation with the landlord).

- The landlord is the Crown or a government department. However, tenants of the Crown Estate Commissioners are protected by the Rent Act.
- Public sector landlords – tenants of local councils, housing associations, housing trusts, new towns, the Housing Corporation, housing co-operatives and other public housing bodies have their own legal protection and are not covered by the Rent Act (see page 90).
- Assured tenancies (see page 58).
- Lettings where the main purpose of the tenant is to carry on a business.
- Lettings where the tenant shares living accommodation with the landlord. This means sharing a kitchen or living room. Only sharing a bathroom or WC does not count. Sharing living accommodation with other tenants does not automatically reduce your protection.
- Lettings where the tenant is a company rather than a person.
- Tenancies that lose their Rent Act protection.

A tenancy may have Rent Act protection but then lose it because a closing or demolition order is put on the property by the local council, because it is illegally overcrowded (see page 149), or because the tenancy agreement has ended and the tenant is no longer using the premises as his/her home.

In addition to these exemptions there is also a form of tenancy known as a shorthold tenancy. For an agreement that states the tenant is a shorthold tenant, see page 75.

Most ordinary tenants of non-resident private landlords whose tenancy began before 15 January 1989 do not fall into any of these exempted categories and are regulated tenants with full Rent Act protection. They have the right to have a fair rent fixed (see page 106), to protection from eviction, and have a wide range of other rights.

The next section describes the rights to protection from eviction of regulated tenants with full Rent Act protection.

For details of the rights of:

- tenants whose letting began on or after 15 January 1989, see page 58
- other tenants, see pages 75–89.

Regulated tenants: protection from eviction

Only tenancies that began before 15 January 1989 and do not come into any of the exempted categories listed above can be regulated tenancies.

Regulated tenants can only be evicted on very limited grounds that are set out in law. They do not have to leave just because the landlord gives them notice to quit, or because the tenancy agreement has run out. Anyone whose landlord asks them to leave should get advice immediately.

The course of action the landlord must take if s/he wants a tenant to leave depends on the type of regulated tenancy that exists.

Is the regulated tenancy 'contractual' or 'statutory'?

Regulated tenancies can be either contractual or statutory. All tenancies start with some form of agreement between the landlord and the tenant. This agreement is a contract and it can be in writing or verbal. This is a contractual tenancy. The contract can be one of two types:

- a fixed-term tenancy, for example, for six months or a year
- a periodic tenancy, meaning that there is no fixed end to the tenancy and rent is paid periodically, usually either weekly or monthly.

Ending the tenancy

A fixed-term tenancy comes to an end automatically at the end of the time specified in the agreement. A periodic tenancy continues indefinitely from week to week or month to month and the landlord can only bring it to an end if s/he serves a Notice to Quit in the proper legal form (see below).

When either a periodic or fixed-term tenancy comes to an end, the tenant does not have to leave, because it automatically becomes what is known as a statutory tenancy. This means that, although the contract between the landlord and tenant has ended, the tenancy still continues on substantially the same terms as before and with the protection of the Rent Act, as long as the tenant continues to live there.

Notice to Quit

Where the landlord wants to seek a possession order against a periodic tenant, s/he must first give the tenant a Notice to Quit in the proper legal form. It must be in writing and give at least four weeks' notice, or longer if the rent is paid at longer intervals. It should expire on a rent day or the day before a rent day. It must also tell the tenants that they do not have to leave unless the landlord gets a court order, and must give information on where to get advice. If the Notice to Quit is not in this form then it has no legal force and the landlord cannot take any further action until a proper notice has been served.

Grounds for eviction

If the tenancy is for a fixed term and it has not yet expired, the landlord can only go to court for a possession order if the tenant has broken one of the terms of the tenancy agreement and the agreement specifies that the tenancy can be ended for that reason. The landlord must also prove it is reasonable for the court to grant a possession order.

If the tenancy agreement is for an indefinite period (a periodic tenancy), the landlord must first bring the tenancy to an end by a Notice to Quit. Once the Notice to Quit has expired and the tenancy has become a statutory tenancy (see above), the landlord can try to persuade the court to grant a possession order against the tenant. Any tenant will only have to leave if the court grants an order to the landlord.

The landlord must prove one of the grounds for possession set out in the Rent Act 1977 to get such an order against a regulated tenant. The first set of grounds are known as discretionary cases. This means that the court may grant a possession order but only if the landlord can prove the ground and if the court thinks that it is reasonable to grant an order. The court also has the power to suspend any possession order, either for a fixed period or indefinitely, subject to certain conditions, for example, the court might make an order for possession because of rent arrears, but suspend the order to give the tenant an opportunity to pay off the arrears. Then, as long as the tenant pays off the agreed amounts, the order will not take effect.

The discretionary grounds for possession are:

Case 1 The tenant is in rent arrears or has broken some other term of the tenancy.

Case 2 The tenant, or someone else living in the home, has caused a nuisance or annoyance to neighbours or has been convicted of using the property for immoral or illegal purposes.

Case 3 The tenant, or someone else living in the home, has damaged or neglected the property.

Case 4 The tenant, or someone living in the home, has damaged furniture provided by the landlord.

Case 5 The landlord has made a contract to sell or let the property because the tenant gave notice that s/he was giving up the tenancy.

Case 6 The tenant has assigned or sublet the whole of the property to another person without the landlord's consent. See page 82 for more details of the law governing subletting and assignment.

Case 7 This has been repealed.

Case 8 The tenant was an employee of the landlord, has now left that employment and the landlord reasonably requires the property for a new employee. (For further details of the rights of people whose homes go with their job, see page 77.)

Case 9 The property is reasonably required by the landlord as a home for him/herself, for any child over 18, or for parents or parents-in-law. But this case does not normally apply if the landlord purchased the property with tenants already in occupation. The tenant can, as a defence against this case, seek to prove that greater hardship would be caused to the tenant by granting the order, than to the landlord by refusing it. In practice, it is very difficult for landlords to use this case as a ground for a possession order.

Case 10 The rent for the property has been fixed by a Rent Officer or Rent Tribunal and the tenant has charged a subtenant more than is allowed under the Rent Act (see page 106 for details of what rents can be charged).

Landlords can also seek possession if they can prove that suitable alternative accommodation is available to the tenant. This might be an offer of accommodation from the local council, or of another property owned by the landlord. In deciding whether the alternative accommodation offered is suitable, the court will take into account the type and size of accommodation, its suitability for the tenant, its distance from work, its cost, the degree of security it offers, and its similarity to the present home. The court must consider whether the accommodation is suitable and also consider that it is reasonable to grant a possession order. It is not easy for landlords to satisfy courts on both these points.

In all cases where the court has discretion whether or not to grant a possession order (that is, in Cases 1–10 (above) and in the case of an offer of suitable alternative accommodation), the court may well refuse to grant an order. In Cases 1–10 (above) the court may grant a suspended order. So, for example, if you can show that you will be able to pay off rent arrears over a reasonable period of time, as long as you stick to this agreement, there is no danger of eviction. So even if one of the discretionary grounds does apply to you it is often worth arguing that it would be unreasonable to grant the order or that it should be suspended.

The second set of grounds for possession are known as mandatory cases. This means that if the landlord can prove that one of these grounds exists, the court must grant a possession order and cannot suspend it for more than 14 days unless there would be exceptional hardship, in which case the maximum is six weeks. In all mandatory cases the landlord must give a written notice at the start of the tenancy (before the grant of the tenancy in Case 19) that s/he might seek a possession order under that case.

The mandatory grounds for possession are:

Case 11 The landlord has let his/her own home and intends to return to live there at a future date. This case can also be used if the owner needs to sell with vacant possession to buy a home nearer to a place of work. If the owner dies, a member of the family who was previously living with him/her and who wishes to live there, can also regain possession, either if they want to live in it, or if they want to sell it with vacant possession. If there is a mortgage on the property, the owner has defaulted on mortgage payments and the lenders wish to sell with vacant possession, the landlord can also use this case.

Case 12 The landlord let accommodation that s/he intends to occupy on retirement. If the owner dies or if a mortgage lender wishes to repossess the property, the same provisions apply as in Case 11.

Case 13 The property was let for a fixed term of not more than eight months and it had been occupied as a holiday letting within the previous 12 months (see page 60 for the definition of a holiday letting).

Case 14 The letting was for a fixed-term of not more than 12 months and it had been occupied as a student letting during the preceding 12 months (see page 92 for the definition of a student letting).

Case 15 The accommodation had been let temporarily but is intended for letting to a minister of religion.

Cases 16, 17 and 18 These relate to various circumstances where properties are normally let to farm workers and have been let temporarily to ordinary tenants.

Case 19 The property was let on a protected shorthold tenancy and that tenancy has come to an end. For further details of protected shorthold tenancies see below.

Case 20 The landlord was a member of the armed forces at the time the tenancy started and intended to live in the house in the future. If the owner dies, a member of the family who was previously living with him/her and who wishes to live there again, can also regain possession under this case. Anyone who inherits the property can regain possession under this case either if they want to live in it, or if they want to sell it with vacant possession. If there is a mortgage on the property, the lenders can use this case if they wish to sell with vacant possession. The case can also be used if the owner needs to sell with vacant possession to buy a home nearer to a place of work.

It is important to remember that the landlord must serve notice on the tenant at the beginning of the tenancy for any of these cases to apply. However, in cases 11 (returning owner-occupier), 12 (retirement home), 19 (shorthold) and 20 (armed forces landlord) the court may grant possession even if the landlord has not fulfilled some of the necessary conditions if it thinks it is just and equitable to do so. The court could therefore decide to waive the rule requiring the landlord to serve notice on the tenant at the start of the tenancy.

Protected shorthold tenancies

For a tenancy to be a protected shorthold, a number of conditions must be fulfilled:

- It must have started on or after 28 November 1980 and before 15 January 1989. After 15 January 1989 new shorthold tenancies are assured shortholds (see page 65). There are now very few protected shorthold tenancies.

- It must be for a fixed period of between one and five years.
- At the start of the tenancy the landlord must have given the tenant a notice in exactly the form laid down in law. The notice informs tenants of the fact that they are taking a shorthold and explains some (but not all) of their rights.
- The Rent Officer must have registered a fair rent for the accommodation (see page 106). However, shortholds outside London that began on or after 1 December 1981 and those in London that began on or after 4 May 1987 do not have to have a fair rent registered, although tenants are still entitled to apply to have a fair rent registered if they wish.
- An existing tenancy could not, under any circumstances, be converted into a shorthold tenancy.

Protected shorthold tenancies: protection from eviction

During the fixed term, the shorthold is the same as any other fixed-term tenancy – the landlord can only seek a possession order if the tenant breaks the terms of the agreement and the contract allows the landlord to seek possession in those circumstances. At the end of the fixed term, if the landlord takes no action to get you out, you have the right to stay for at least an extra year. If the landlord wants to regain possession at the end of the fixed term, s/he must follow a fairly complex procedure. The landlord must give notice in writing during the last three months of the tenancy. The notice must give at least three months' warning of his/her intention to seek a possession order in the court. Then, after that notice has expired, the landlord must apply to the court within three months of the date given in the notice.

If the agreed shorthold period expires and the landlord has not served a notice on the tenant that s/he intends to seek a possession order, then s/he has to wait another nine months before being able to serve such a notice. Similarly, if the landlord serves a notice of his/her intention to seek possession, and then does not actually apply to the court in the three months allowed, s/he has to wait another nine months before being able to serve such a notice.

Once the case comes to court, the landlord will have to prove that the tenancy was a valid shorthold and that the proper notice procedure has been followed. However, the court can overlook a failure to follow two of the conditions if it considers it is just and equitable to do so. The two conditions it may overlook are:

- the requirement that a notice be given to the tenant in the prescribed form stating that the letting is a shorthold

- the requirement that a fair rent be registered or a certificate of fair rent issued at the correct time.

This section only applies to protected shorthold tenancies created before 15 January 1989. After that date different provisions apply to newly created assured shorthold tenancies (see page 65).

Tied housing: a home with a job

Some people take a job that includes accommodation, for example a caretaker or a pub manager. This section deals with tied tenants in the private sector whenever they began. Tenants in the public sector are dealt with on page 90 and agricultural workers in tied housing on page 78. People in tied housing may be either licensees (known as service occupiers), or tenants (known as service tenants), depending on their circumstances. The difference between the two is not defined in legislation but is based on judgments in court cases.

However, just because an employer and a landlord are the same person it does not mean that a tenant automatically lives in tied housing. S/he might, for example, be an ordinary private tenant who was offered a job by their landlord. This would not by itself turn him/her into a tied tenant. The landlord has to prove that the home was taken in consequence of the job. Generally this means that the tenant takes up home and job together and that there is some connection between the two. If there is no such connection, the tenant is an ordinary tenant or licensee.

Service occupiers: in order for your landlord to prove that you are merely a licensee, or service occupier, it must be shown that:

- either it is necessary for you to live in the accommodation in order to carry out your duties
- your contract of employment requires you to live there and it is necessary for the better performance of your duties.

So, for example, it might be argued that it was necessary for a caretaker to live on the premises for security reasons. It is not enough simply to show that it is more convenient, for example because it is nearer to the place of work. If you are a service occupier who has exclusive possession of your home (see page 57 for what 'exclusive possession' means) then the landlord can only evict you by going to court for a possession order. You cannot just be told to leave.

Service tenants: if the letting was in consequence of the job but is not necessary in either of the two ways listed above, then you are probably a service tenant. Service tenants have many of the same rights as ordinary tenants and their security depends on whether they are assured tenants (see page 58), fully protected, or only have basic security (see page 81). If the tenancy began before 15 January 1989 there is, however, an additional ground for eviction in the Rent Act, where the tenant has left the landlord's employment and the landlord now reasonably requires the property for a new employee (see page 72). If the tenancy began on or after 15 January 1989, there is an additional ground for possession in the Housing Act 1988 (see page 64).

Tied housing: agricultural workers

This section applies to tenancies that began before 15 January 1989. If a tenancy began on or after that date see page 67. Agricultural workers have special protection under the Rent (Agriculture) Act 1976, which added a complex layer to existing legislation. This section gives a brief outline of the protection available. Farm workers worried about losing their homes should get advice from their union or a housing advice centre.

The basis of the 1976 Act is that it gives security to those agricultural workers who are not protected by the Rent Act 1977.

These occupiers are protected until suitable alternative accommodation is available and the Act puts obligations on local councils to help with alternative accommodation. To qualify for these benefits, you must be in accommodation provided by your employer and have been working full time in agriculture for at least 91 weeks out of any period of 104 weeks during the period of your occupation. Farm workers employed and housed by government departments, the Crown or certain other public bodies, are not covered by the Act, but administrative arrangements have been made to give them broadly the same benefits.

Agricultural workers: protected occupiers

In order to qualify for protection the occupier must have a tenancy or licence that meets certain conditions. If you have a licence (see page 56) it must be one that allows exclusive occupation of the property and which, if it had been a tenancy, would have had Rent Act protection.

If you have a tenancy, again it must be of the kind that would have Rent Act protection. For the purposes of this Act, the following types of arrangement would also be included as being equivalent to lettings with Rent Act protection:

- lettings to occupiers who pay no, or low rent
- lettings of property on an agricultural holding
- lettings where meals are provided in the course of employment and where any attendance provided is not substantial (see page 68 for what is meant by 'attendances' and 'substantial').

With these exceptions, the lettings must meet all the conditions that bring a tenancy within the Rent Act (see page 67 for a full description of these). Occupiers who meet these criteria have a protected occupancy. Agricultural workers who have a resident landlord, and those who live in hostels, are not protected occupiers.

In order to gain possession from a protected occupier the employer must prove one of the following grounds:

Case 1 Suitable alternative accommodation has been offered by a landlord other than the local authority.

Case 2 Alternative accommodation has been offered by the local authority.

Case 3 Rent arrears, or breaking other conditions of the tenancy or licence agreement.

Case 4 Causing a nuisance, or using the property for illegal purposes.

Case 5 Damaging the property.

Case 6 Damaging the furniture provided by the landlord.

Case 7 The tenant has given notice to quit.

Case 8 The tenant has illegally assigned, sublet, or parted with possession of the property.

Case 9 The landlord wants the property to live in, either personally, or for his/her family, and it was purchased before 13 April 1976.

Case 10 Overcharging of subtenant.

Case 11 A returning owner-occupier.

Case 12 The property is intended as a retirement home.

Case 13 Overcrowding.

The details of these grounds for possession are similar to the Rent Act grounds (see page 72).

Cases 1–10 are discretionary, meaning that the landlord must prove the case, and the court must think it is reasonable to grant possession. Cases 11–13 are mandatory, meaning that if the case is proved, the court must grant possession.

If the landlord wishes to gain possession, s/he can apply to the local council for suitable alternative accommodation for the occupier. The landlord must show that the property is required in order that a new employee can be housed, that s/he cannot provide alternative accommodation, and that the local council should provide alternative accommodation 'in the interests of efficient agriculture'. There is a procedure for the local council, the landlord, or the occupier to refer the case to a local Agricultural Dwelling House Advisory Committee to advise on the issues involved. Where the council is satisfied of the applicant's case it must use its best endeavours to provide alternative accommodation.

Farm workers not protected by the Rent (Agriculture) Act 1976

Where an agricultural worker is not a protected occupier under the Act, there are special provisions under the Protection from Eviction Act 1977 to give some limited rights. The court has special powers to suspend a possession order and, if the order is made within six months of the end of the tenancy or licence, the order must be suspended until the end of that six-month period unless suitable alternative accommodation will be available, or there are other strong reasons for not suspending it.

Since 15 January 1989, assured tenancies that began before this date have been subject to the provisions of the Housing Act 1988 (see page 65).

Tenants with only basic protection

Tenants who have only basic protection are those who are excluded from full protection. This will normally be because:

- The tenant is provided with substantial board, for example meals (see page 68) and the tenancy began before 15 January 1989.

- The tenant has a resident landlord and does not share any rooms with the landlord. (If you share any accommodation with the landlord you are known as an 'excluded occupier' and do not have even basic protection.)

In most cases, the landlord still has to get a possession order from the court in order to evict you and any other attempt at eviction is illegal. If there is a fixed-term agreement the landlord cannot evict you before the agreement has expired unless you break the agreement. If there is no fixed-term agreement the landlord must give a Notice to Quit in the proper form (see page 71) before going to court. However, some tenants and licensees are excluded from this protection (see page 156).

Sharers

People who share a rented home often regard themselves as having equal legal rights in it. But, in fact, their legal positions may be quite different and can be very complicated. They could be tenants, subtenants, licensees or a combination of these.

Joint tenants

The simplest position is where the group of sharers all took the tenancy together and where all their names are on the tenancy agreement or rent book. They hold as a group and individually all the rights and responsibilities of individual tenants. So, for example, they are jointly and individually responsible for keeping to the tenancy agreement and paying the rent. If one tenant fails to pay their share of the rent, the others will be equally responsible for any arrears. They have the same protection from eviction as individual tenants in the same circumstances.

However, complications can arise if one of the tenants leaves and is replaced by a different person. The best approach is to agree the replacement with the landlord. If this is not done the new sharer may be only a subtenant or even a licensee of the remaining tenants.

Subtenants

If a tenant of a property sublets all or part of it to someone else, that person is known as a subtenant. The legal position can become very complicated because there are now three sets of relationships involved: landlord and tenant; tenant and subtenant; and landlord and subtenant. This section gives a broad outline of the legal position but anyone in doubt about their status should get legal advice.

If the tenancy began before 15 January 1989 a tenant is allowed to sublet a part of the property if this is not forbidden in the tenancy agreement. If the tenancy is an assured tenancy that began on or after 15 January 1989, then a tenant is not allowed to sublet without the landlord's agreement. In practice, most agreements do prohibit subletting and any subtenancies created despite the prohibition, are known as illegal subtenancies. Even if subletting is prohibited, however, it may be possible to have people staying simply as lodgers or licensees, unless this is also forbidden in the agreement (it may, for example, forbid taking in 'paying guests'). A regulated tenant can be evicted if s/he sublets all of the property without the landlord's consent.

When subletting is forbidden

If subletting is prohibited but you do it anyway, the landlord will have a case for seeking a possession order. However, if you can show that the landlord knew about the subtenant and took no action, it may be possible to argue that tacit consent had been given. If you change your mind and want to evict the subtenant, you cannot do so on the grounds that the original subletting was illegal (although you may have other grounds for a possession order).

When subletting is not forbidden

If subletting is not forbidden and you consider doing so, you will need to make sure that the subletting does not create overcrowding (see page 149). You must also ensure that the subtenant does not damage the landlord's property or furniture, or cause a nuisance to neighbours. In addition, if you are a regulated tenant, you must not charge more than is allowed under the Rent Act (see page 106). If any of these things happen then these could be grounds for the landlord to seek a possession order against you.

If you are not a regulated tenant, subletting without the knowledge and full consent of the landlord would be most inadvisable since your landlord can evict you.

The subtenant's protection from eviction

As long as the tenant continues to hold the tenancy, then s/he is the landlord of the subtenant. The security of the subtenant is decided in the same way as for any other tenant. In most instances the tenant is a resident landlord and the subtenant will usually have only basic protection if they do not share any rooms with the main tenant, or no protection if they do share rooms (see page 82).

Even if subletting is forbidden, the landlord cannot evict the subtenant without evicting the tenant at the same time. If the tenant is evicted or gives up the tenancy, then the subtenant's position depends first on whether or not subletting was forbidden. If subletting was forbidden then, once the tenant has gone, the landlord can normally evict the subtenant. If subletting was not forbidden then the subtenant's security depends on the degree of protection enjoyed by the tenant, and by the subtenant in relation to the tenant. In the unlikely event that the subtenant was fully protected in relation to a protected tenant, if the tenant leaves, the subtenant becomes the direct, fully protected tenant of the landlord. If either the subtenant or the tenant was not fully protected then the landlord can normally evict the subtenant once the tenant has left. The position of assured tenants is similar. If an assured tenant's immediate landlord is the tenant of another landlord and the immediate landlord's tenancy comes to an end, the subtenant becomes the assured tenant of the head landlord.

Sharers who are licensees

It is common in flat shares for one person to be named on the tenancy agreement and for this person to take responsibility for dealings with the landlord. There is usually no written agreement between this person and the other sharers. In these circumstances it is quite likely that they are not joint tenants. The other sharers may be subtenants or merely licensees of the tenant who deals with the landlord. It is often difficult to establish the legal status of flat sharers but the informality of many flat-sharing arrangements, where people split household bills and even food costs (rather than having the formal arrangement typical of landlords and tenants), suggests that the sharers may simply be the licensees of the tenant named on the agreement with the landlord. However, if it can be demonstrated that the sharers live as separate households, this would tend to suggest subtenancies. The dividing line between a tenancy and a licence is not clear (see page 56) but sharers are not necessarily all licensees just because none of them has exclusive occupation of one part of the flat. If they rented the flat from the landlord as a group with only one tenancy agreement for all of them, they will probably be joint tenants. As can be seen, these cases are often very complex and anyone in this position should seek legal advice.

Tenants of landlords with mortgages

Many tenants have landlords who have a mortgage on the property that was taken out before the tenancy began. Most mortgage agreements prohibit letting and these tenants are in a similar position to illegal subtenants. In relation to their landlord they will have the same degree of protection as any other tenant, but in relation to the lender, the tenant has no protection. So if the lender repossesses the property, the tenant can be evicted.

If, however, the mortgage was taken out after the tenant became a tenant of the property, his/her security will not be affected. If the lender repossesses the property from the landlord, they also take over his/her position in relation to the tenant, and the tenant's degree of legal protection remains the same. However, in practice most mortgage companies will require any existing tenant or occupier to waive their rights against the mortgage company before granting a mortgage. This does not affect the tenant's rights in relation to the owner of the property, but will remove any rights the tenant might have had in relation to the mortgage company if it wants to repossess the property.

Licensees: protection from eviction

The difference between a licensee and a tenant is explained on page 56.

Many licensees come within the Protection from Eviction Act 1977, which means that the landlord must give them proper notice and get a court order before evicting them. For further details see page 155. If your licence agreement is not for a fixed period, and it is not one of those excluded from the Protection from Eviction Act (see page 156), then the landlord must give you written notice to quit of at least four weeks in the proper legal form.

Going to court

When the landlord wants to take you to court to evict you, the next step after the Notice to Quit (if one is required, see page 156), or Notice of Possession Proceedings (see page 61), or a Notice Ending a Licence, is that you will receive a court summons. In most cases you will also receive a form that allows you to either admit the landlord's case, or to state your defence. If you wish to, you can also make a claim against the landlord (known as a counterclaim), for example for damages for any repairs that have not been made. This form should be returned to the court within 14 days. If you have not yet sought legal advice, do so immediately and get help in filling in the form before returning it. If you fail to return the form within the 14 days, return it as soon as possible after that with an explanation for the delay.

If you have sent in a defence, the first court hearing may be a case management hearing, at which the judge will set down a timetable for the preparations for the trial. If you have good reasons for not having had a chance to submit a defence, you can ask for a chance to do this and for the case to be heard at a later date. However, you cannot use this simply as a delaying tactic, and you may also find that you have to pay the landlord's legal costs for that day, regardless of the outcome of the case. These costs may be considerable.

When the case comes to court, you can speak for yourself, but courts can be very intimidating and your chances may be better if you can get a solicitor or barrister to represent you. However close it is to the court hearing, you may still be able to win the case. If the case has already been to court and you think a mistaken judgment has been given, you may be able to appeal against it. Get advice as soon as possible. You may qualify for public funding (formerly known as Legal Aid) to help with any costs (see page 184).

If the judge grants a possession order, you or your representative might be able to ask for it to be suspended. It can be suspended either for a fixed period, or indefinitely with conditions attached. If it is suspended, be sure that you fully understand fully conditions the judge makes, for example how much of any arrears you must pay off each week. Do not agree to pay off more than you can afford. If you find you cannot meet the conditions, it is possible to go back to the court to ask for them to be changed, although the judge may not necessarily agree to this. If you have met all the conditions (for example, paying off all the arrears), you can go back to court to ask for the order to be discharged. It is a good idea to do this because it prevents the landlord using it against you in the future.

The judge will usually postpone the date on which you must give possession of the property for a short period. In most cases, this period is at the judge's discretion and 28 days is fairly common. However, in certain cases (notably assured shorthold tenancies, where the court is obliged to grant an order if the case is proved), the court normally only allows 14 days, with a maximum of six weeks in cases of exceptional hardship. See page 65 for details of assured shorthold tenancies.

In addition to these normal procedures, in certain very limited circumstances, there are special procedures for speedier evictions. Assured shorthold tenants can be evicted by such a procedure. The tenant is sent a copy of an affidavit prepared by the landlord that sets out the reasons for seeking possession. If the tenant agrees with it, or fails to respond within 14 days, the landlord can ask the court to order possession. If the tenant disputes the accuracy of the landlord's case, an ordinary court hearing will normally take place. Any tenant threatened with eviction in this way should get advice immediately. See page 65 for details of assured shorthold tenancies.

An even quicker procedure is available for use against trespassers who are either squatters, or licensees whose licence has been ended by the landlord.

The landlord can arrange for a court hearing without even knowing the names of the occupiers. Normally not less than five days' notice of the hearing is given, but the court can allow an even shorter period. Normally the possession order is not postponed, but where the occupiers were originally licensees the court can postpone the order.

Eviction

When the date for possession has arrived, the next step is that the landlord can apply to the court for a warrant of possession that enables the bailiffs, who are court officers, to carry out the eviction. The bailiffs must give notice of the eviction.

If the possession order is suspended on certain conditions (for example, payment of arrears) and those conditions are broken, the landlord does not normally have to go back to the judge, but can go straight to the bailiffs for eviction. If this happens, you can go to court to get the eviction stopped. You will need immediate legal advice to do this as you may only have a few days.

Illegal evictions and harassment

If the landlord tries to get you out by any other means than the legal steps defined in this section, s/he is acting illegally. See page 155 for more details of protection from harassment and illegal eviction.

The key questions for private tenants

The law relating to protection from eviction for private tenants is complicated. The key questions to answer are:

- Are you a licensee or a tenant (page 56)?
- If you are a tenant are you:

- – an assured tenant (page 58)
- – an assured shorthold tenant (page 65)
- – an excluded occupier (page 66)
- – a regulated tenant (page 67)
- – a protected shorthold tenant (page 75)
- – a service tenant (page 78)
- – a tenant with only basic protection (page 81)
- – a subtenant (page 82)
- – a joint tenant (page 82)
- – a tenant of a mortgagor (page 85)?
- If you are a licensee, are you:
  - – a service occupier (page 77)?
- If you are an agricultural worker, do you qualify for protection under the Rent (Agriculture) Act 1976 or the Housing Act 1988 (pages 78 and 58)?

If you are in any doubt about your position see Chapter 7.

Council tenants, housing association tenants and tenants of other public landlords

The majority of council, housing association and other tenants of public sector landlords have protection from eviction. Their landlords can only evict if they can prove to a court that one of a number of grounds for possession exists. Normally tenants who pay their rent and do not break the tenancy agreement are completely secure in their homes. However, the Housing Act 1996 brought in a new introductory tenancy that local authorities can use for the first year of new tenancies. For details see page 97.

Housing association tenants

If your tenancy began before 15 January 1989, the following sections for secure tenants are the most relevant. If your tenancy began on or after 15 January 1989, you will be covered by the provisions on assured tenancies found in the Housing Act 1996 (see page 58).

Secure tenants

The majority of council tenants (and housing association tenants whose tenancy began before 15 January 1989) are secure. Unlike in the private sector, licensees have the same legal protection as tenants. The only exceptions are:

- where they are being housed temporarily because they have been accepted by the local council as homeless
- where they have been given an introductory tenancy by the local council (see page 97)
- residents in hostels provided by councils and housing associations – these people do not have protection from eviction
- where they first entered their home as squatters and were then given a temporary licence for that or another property by the landlord. These ex-squatter licensees do not have the same protection as tenants.

Tenants of all the following landlords count as secure tenants:

- a local authority
- the Housing Corporation
- a housing trust that is registered as a charity
- a new town development corporation
- the Commission for the New Towns
- the Development Board for Rural Wales
- a housing co-operative where the properties are owned by the local council (tenants of co-operatives where the properties are owned by the co-op itself are not secure tenants)

- an urban development corporation
- a housing association registered with the Housing Corporation, or with an application for registration pending (but not co-ownership associations) if the tenancy began before 15 January 1989. If your tenancy began after that date, see page 58.

A tenant of the Crown (someone who rents a property that belongs to the Queen, a government department or is held in trust for the Queen) is not a secure tenant, but many do have some legal protection. In order to be secure, the tenant must be a person (not a company) and the property must be their only or main home.

There is a long list of types of public tenancy that are excluded from security, but the actual numbers of tenants involved are very small. The exclusions are:

- Long leases of more than 21 years.
- Tied accommodation where the contract of employment requires the tenant to occupy his/her home for the better performance of his/her duties, and is employed by the landlord or by a local authority, a new town development corporation, the Commission for the New Towns, the Development Board for Rural Wales, or an urban development corporation.
- The tenant is a member of the police force and the home is provided rent free.
- The tenant works for the fire brigade, and the contract of employment requires him/her to live close to a fire station and the home was let so s/he could do so.
- Tied accommodation where the tenant is employed by the landlord and the tenancy agreement states that the tenancy will end at the same time as the employment ends, and that the accommodation is held by the landlord for educational or social services purposes and is part of, or within the grounds of, an educational or social services building. This covers accommodation for people such as school caretakers and residential social workers.

- Almshouses.
- A tenancy given to the tenant because s/he has applied for housing as a homeless person and has the tenancy on a temporary basis.
- Temporary accommodation given to the tenant for less than a year so that s/he could move to take up a job in that area, or a neighbouring area. The landlord must notify the tenant at the beginning of the tenancy that it is on this basis.
- The landlord has leased the property from a private landlord and then sublet to the tenant on a temporary basis.
- Temporary accommodation provided to the tenant while work is carried out on his/her usual home and the tenant is not a secure tenant in his/her usual home.
- Student lettings where the tenant is attending a course that has been designated for this purpose by the Government. The landlord must notify the tenant at the beginning of the tenancy that it is on this basis.
- Business tenancies, agricultural holdings and licensed premises.
- Homes on land acquired for redevelopment and those being used for temporary housing. This covers, for example, short-life housing (see page 48).

Protection from eviction for secure tenants

The majority of public sector tenants are secure and can only be evicted on very limited grounds. If the landlord believes that one of these grounds exists, the first thing they must do is give you a notice, usually known as a Notice of Intended Proceedings or a Notice of Seeking Possession, and this notice must tell you the grounds on which the landlord is seeking to evict you. It should normally give a date, at least four weeks ahead, after which the case may be taken to court. The notice only remains in force for one year after that date. It then lapses and if the landlord wants to try again to evict you, they will have to give you a new notice. The court can, however, decide that a notice was not necessary if it is just and equitable to do so.

Once the date given on the notice has passed, the next step is for the landlord to go to court to prove one of the grounds for possession set out below applies to you. The first six grounds are discretionary, which means that the court may grant a possession order but only if the landlord can prove the case and the court thinks that it is reasonable to grant an order. The court also has the power to suspend any possession order, either for a fixed period, or indefinitely, subject to certain conditions. For example, the court might make an order for possession because of rent arrears but suspend the order to give you an opportunity to pay them off. As long as you pay off the agreed amount, the order will not take effect. Public sector landlords generally do not wish to evict tenants. So if, for example, they do get a possession order for rent arrears, they may choose not to go ahead with the eviction straight away, to give you a chance to pay off the arrears.

The discretionary grounds for possession are:

Ground 1 The tenant has rent arrears or has broken any obligation in the tenancy agreement.

Ground 2 The tenant, or anyone living with him/her, or visiting the home, has caused a nuisance or annoyance to neighbours or other people visiting the area, or has been convicted of using the property for illegal or immoral purposes, or committed an offence in the neighbourhood.

Ground 2A The tenants are a married couple living together as husband and wife or are civil partners and one has left because of violence or the threat of violence against him/her or a member of the family, and s/he is unlikely to return.

Ground 3 The tenant, or anyone living with him/her, damages the property or part of the building shared with other tenants.

Ground 4 The tenant, or anyone living with him/her, damages furniture provided by the landlord.

Ground 5 You got the tenancy by knowingly or recklessly making false statements to the landlord, or getting somebody else to make such statements.

Ground 6 The tenant exchanged his/her home with another tenant and either paid money to, or received money from, the other tenant as a condition of making the exchange.

Ground 7 The home goes with the job, it is part of larger premises that are not used mainly for housing (for example, a school) and someone living in the tenancy is guilty of misconduct that would make it not right for him/her to continue to live there.

Ground 8 The tenant has been moved to another property while building work is carried out on the home and s/he refuses to leave the temporary accommodation to return to the original home.

For the next three grounds for possession, the court must grant a possession order if the landlord can prove the case, but the landlord must also prove that suitable alternative accommodation is available (see below for what counts as suitable alternative accommodation). These grounds are:

Ground 9 The tenant breaks the law by overcrowding the home (see page 149 for what counts as illegal overcrowding).

Ground 10 The landlord wants to demolish the building or carry out work on it, and cannot do so while it is occupied.

Ground 10A The home is in an area for which there is a redevelopment scheme and the landlord plans, as part of the scheme, to sell the property. If the landlord wants to use this ground for possession, they must give details of their plans, allow the tenant at least 28 days to comment on them and then take his/her views into account. The redevelopment scheme must be approved by the Secretary of State or, where the landlord is a registered housing association, by the Housing Corporation. If a tenant is evicted on this ground s/he will be eligible for a home loss payment (see page 21) as well as being entitled to suitable alternative accommodation.

Ground 11 The landlord is a charity and occupation of the property conflicts with the objects of the charity. For example, the charity's objectives may be to help people with disabilities and there may be no one with a disability living in the accommodation.

For the next five grounds for possession the court may grant a possession order only if it considers both that it is reasonable to do so and that suitable alternative accommodation is available. These grounds for possession are:

Ground 12 The home was let to the tenant in consequence of his/her employment, it is part of premises not mainly used for housing, the tenant no longer works in that job and the landlord needs the property for another employee.

Ground 13 The property has been specially designed for a person with a physical disability, there is no one with a disability living there and the landlord needs it for such a tenant.

Ground 14 The landlord is a housing association or housing trust that lets only to special groups of people who have difficulty in getting housing, there is no longer such a person living there or the tenant has received an offer of a secure tenancy from the local council, and the landlord needs the accommodation for a person from the special groups for which it caters. The special groups could include people with, for example, particular disabilities, but this ground does not cover associations that let to people because of their low income and could not be used to evict someone because they were no longer on a low income.

Ground 15 The property is one of a group let to people with particular needs and is near a special facility (for example, an old people's club); there is no longer such a person living there and the council needs the property for someone with those special needs.

Ground 16 The previous tenant has died, a member of the family has taken over the tenancy and the home is larger than s/he needs. The landlord can only seek possession on this ground between six and 12 months after the tenant's death and it cannot be used against the widow or widower or civil partner of the previous tenant, or against someone who was a joint tenant with the person who has died. In deciding whether it is reasonable to grant a possession order on this ground the court has to take into account the age of the remaining tenant, how long s/he has lived there and any financial or other support given by him/her to the previous tenant.

Where the landlord has to prove that suitable alternative accommodation is available, this has to be an offer of another home that is suitable, taking account of where the tenant works, where his/her children go to school and whether it is essential that s/he lives close to a family member. Whether the offer is suitable can depend on the types of home being let to other people in the area (for example, if there are a larger number of flats in the area, a flat rather than a house may be offered). But it is the court that decides whether or not the alternative accommodation is suitable and a tenant can dispute the landlord's offer in court if s/he thinks it is not.

There are many ways in which a tenant can defend him/herself in court. If the landlord has not served a proper Notice of Seeking Possession they are not entitled to proceed with the case unless the court decides it is just and equitable to proceed, for example because the case has not been damaged by the landlord's error. The landlord must produce evidence supporting the reasons s/he believes s/he is entitled to evict, and the tenant can challenge that evidence. In the cases where they must also prove that it is reasonable to evict, a tenant can argue in court that it is not reasonable. For example, if they have not given the tenant a chance to pay off rent arrears, or to change the behaviour they are complaining about, the tenant could argue it is not reasonable to evict.

If the landlord does not give enough details of the reasons why they think they should have a possession order, the tenant can dispute the case in court.

Even if the court decides to grant a possession order, the judge often decides to suspend it. If, for example, a tenant gets into rent arrears, the court may suspend the order to give the tenant a chance to pay off the arrears. In these circumstances the tenant needs to agree with the landlord and the court a regular amount that will be paid off the arrears. This should be an affordable amount and the court should not try to make the tenant pay off an amount that would cause any exceptional hardship. As long as this agreement is upheld, the threat of eviction should subside.

There have been many cases of tenants successfully defending themselves. Any tenant who receives a Notice of Seeking Possession should get advice immediately, so as to allow as much time as possible to work out a defence. Even if a possession order has been granted against, there is still time to seek advice.

It may be possible to appeal against the order, or at least to delay the eviction. See page 86 for more details on going to court.

Introductory, probationary and demoted tenancies

Local councils and housing associations can also grant tenancies with less protection. These are known as introductory tenancies for council tenants, and probationary tenancies for housing association tenants. The aim is to allow councils and housing associations to take quicker action against antisocial tenants. These tenancies last for 12 months, after which they automatically become secure tenancies for council tenants, or assured tenancies for housing association tenants. However, councils can extend an introductory tenancy for a further six months. If the council wants to evict a tenant from an introductory tenancy, it must serve a notice on the tenant giving its reasons and allowing the tenant 14 days to ask for an internal review. If it decides to go ahead with the eviction it must tell the tenant why and go to court for an order, which the court must grant.

Probationary tenancies for housing association tenants are assured shorthold tenancies.

Local councils and housing associations can also apply to the county court for ordinary tenancies to be 'demoted' for 12 months, to become the equivalent of introductory tenancies and assured shorthold tenancies.

Homeowners

Homeowners have a high degree of security and there are only limited circumstances in which they might lose their homes.

Mortgage arrears

If you do not keep up your mortgage payments the lender will eventually be able to evict you and sell the property to recoup their money. If you have difficulties keeping up the payments see page 117. Even if you are taken to court, you can still try to persuade the judge to grant a suspended possession order to give you a chance to pay off the arrears. If you are in danger of losing your home in this way, seek advice immediately. The number of homeowners who have lost their homes because of mortgage arrears has been increasing. It is important not to over-commit yourself by taking on a mortgage that you can only just afford, and that you could not afford if there was a drop in your income, or an increase in mortgage interest rates.

Action by the local council

In rare circumstances, the council may make a compulsory purchase order on an owner-occupied property. It may do this in order to demolish the property, particularly if it is in a slum clearance area. An inquiry will normally have to be held into any proposal for compulsory purchase, and owners who wish to oppose the plans can get their legal costs paid. Owners (and tenants) who lose their homes in this way have a right to be rehoused by the council and to compensation (see page 21).

Long leaseholders: protection from eviction

Almost all flats and some houses have in the past been owned on long leases rather than outright. Many of these leases will last long beyond the lifetime of the owners, so there is little reason to worry about what happens when they run out. But some leases, particularly on older houses, do run out. When this happens, the leaseholder still has a right to stay indefinitely. However, the landlord can serve a notice that you should become a statutory tenant and you would then stay on paying rent. There is one additional ground for possession under this procedure. If the landlord is a local authority or other public body, they can seek possession if they propose to demolish or reconstruct all or most of the property. However, this ground is rarely used.

Mobile homes

If you own a mobile home, rent a pitch for it on a site and live there as your main home, you are protected by the Mobile Homes Act 1983. (If you rent the home you will be covered by the laws for tenants.) The Act does not however cover you if you only use the home for holidays.

Protection from eviction

The Mobile Homes Act 1983 gives owners the right to keep their homes on the protected site they occupy indefinitely. To be protected, a site must have planning permission to be used as a caravan site and the owner must hold (or be entitled to hold) a site licence from the local authority. There can only be a fixed time limit on the agreement if the site owner's planning permission, or right to use the land, is itself limited to a fixed period. If this time limit is later extended, then so is your right to stay there. The resident can bring the agreement to an end by giving at least four weeks' notice in writing. The site owner can only bring the agreement to an end by applying to the county court or to an arbitrator (see Settling disputes, page 101). There are only three grounds on which the site owner can seek to end an agreement:

- You are not living in the mobile home as your main residence.
- The mobile home is having a detrimental effect on the site because of its condition, or is likely to have this effect within the next five years. The site owner can only try to use this ground for ending the agreement once in any five-year period, starting from the date the agreement began.

- You have broken one of the terms of the agreement and the court or arbitrator thinks it is reasonable to end the agreement. The site owner must first tell you that you have broken the agreement and give you a reasonable time to put things right.

If the site owner can prove to the court or arbitrator that the agreement should be brought to an end for one of these reasons, the site owner can then get an eviction order from the court. Arbitrators cannot make eviction orders. The site owner can normally go to court to ask to end the agreement and for an eviction order at the same time.

If the site is privately owned, the court can suspend an eviction order for up to one year, but cannot suspend it if the site is owned by the local council. It is a criminal offence for the site owner to evict you without a court order; to harass or threaten you; or to cut off services such as gas, electricity or water so as to get you to leave. If you have any of these problems, seek advice.

The site owner can make you move to another part of the site only if:

- your agreement says that this can be done
- the new pitch is broadly comparable to the old one
- the site owner pays all the costs.

The right to a written agreement and to a statement of rights

The site owner must give occupiers and prospective occupiers a written statement of their legal rights and the terms of their agreement. In the case of prospective occupiers, the written statement must be given to them at least 28 days before any agreement for sale is made. This agreement cannot change the rights set out in the Mobile Homes Act. You or the site owner can apply to change the terms of the agreement within six months of the issue of the original written statement. Either side can apply to the county court or to an arbitrator if they cannot agree the terms. Check that the agreement states the amount of pitch fees you will have to pay and the rules about charging these. If you are unhappy with the arrangements for fees you can, as with the rest of the agreement, apply within six months to change them.

You also have protection from harassment and illegal eviction. If the site owner does anything that is likely to interfere with your peace or comfort, or persistently withholds services, they can be prosecuted by the local authority.

Other rights of mobile homeowners

You can sell your home and pass on the agreement with the site owner to a person of your choice. You can also give your home to a member of your family. In either case, the new owner must be approved by the site owner, but the site owner must respond within 28 days and approval cannot be unreasonably withheld. If you think the site owner is withholding approval unreasonably, you can apply to the court or an arbitrator for an order that the site owner must give approval. If you sell your home the site owner can claim a commission of up to ten per cent of the price. If you die, members of your family who were living with you will automatically inherit the agreement with the site owner, along with all your legal rights.

Settling disputes

If you have a dispute with the site owner you can settle this by going either to the county court or to an arbitrator, who is an independent person agreed by both sides. Your written agreement may set out the procedure for appointing an arbitrator. You can only use an arbitrator if both you and the site owner have made a written agreement to do so in the event of a dispute. Otherwise you can go to court. Arbitration can be quicker and cheaper than going to court, but make sure it is in your interests before agreeing to it. Once you have made a written agreement to use an arbitrator, rather than the court, you will be bound by this and you cannot then go to court unless you believe the arbitrator was biased (for example, because s/he was connected with the site owner in some way) or if a mistake was made over the law. If the site owner's proposed written agreement includes the use of arbitration, seek advice before signing it.

Squatters

This section is for people who are squatting or thinking of squatting in premises without the permission of the owner. If you have permission from the owner, whether written or spoken, then you may be either a licensee or a tenant and this section does not apply to you. Squatters who do not have the permission of the owner to live in a property count in law as trespassers. This is not in itself a crime, but it is easy for the owners to evict you very quickly and you may be committing a crime if you do not leave when ordered to do so.

Getting a possession order from the court

Normally, an owner will go to court to get a possession order to evict you. There are special procedures for evicting squatters quickly. The owner does not even have to give your name to the court. The first you hear may be papers from the court giving you the date of the court hearing. This may give as little as five days' notice. The owner can go either to the county court or the High Court. If the court decides that you are trespassing, it can grant an immediate possession order, though you may be able to negotiate with the owner for a delay of perhaps two to four weeks if you agree beforehand not to defend the case in court. Owners will normally use the court bailiffs to carry out the eviction and this would give you a further week or so. You should not obstruct the bailiff in any way because this is a criminal offence.

There is an even faster procedure introduced by the Criminal Justice Act 1994. It applies to squatters who have been in the property for less than 28 days. The landlord can serve a Notice of Possession on the squatters and then get an Interim Possession Order; this gives you only 24 hours to leave the property or risk facing arrest.

Eviction by someone living in or entitled to live in the property

Squatters do not usually want to take someone else's home, but if you do find yourself in this position, you could be committing a criminal offence if the person entitled to live in the property asks you to leave and you refuse. If someone who qualifies as a displaced residential occupier or a protected intending occupier (or someone acting on behalf of either) asks you to leave and you refuse, you could be prosecuted.

- A displaced residential occupier is someone who was living in the property immediately before it was squatted. You would have a defence to any prosecution if you had reasonable grounds for believing that the person had not been living there.
- There are two types of protected intending occupier:

  – owners (including long leaseholders), tenants and licensees who intend to live in the property themselves.

  – people who have been offered a tenancy of the property by a public sector landlord such as a local council or housing association.

When asking you to leave, private sector occupiers, or their representatives, have to present you with a sworn statement that they come into this category. Public sector tenants, or their representatives, have to present you with a certificate from the landlord that the property has been offered to, and accepted by, a protected intending occupier. Private landlords cannot use this provision.

Forcible eviction of squatters

Some owners may use force to evict squatters. If they try to do so they may be committing a criminal offence and you should get advice. However, taking the owner to court will not get you back into the property. Some owners wait until everyone is out and then change the locks on the property. This is not in itself illegal. If you are squatting or thinking of squatting, get advice as soon as possible; it may be too late once the owner has started to evict you.

Paying for your home and reducing your housing costs

3

Introduction

This chapter gives advice on how to pay for your home. There are two main ways of reducing housing costs:

- making sure you are not paying any higher rent, service charges or mortgage repayments than you have to
- claiming any benefits or subsidies to which you might be entitled.

Private tenants

There are a number of ways in which private tenants can reduce their costs and get help with paying for their home:

- If your tenancy began before 15 January 1989 you may be able to get a fair rent registered. Once this is fixed the landlord cannot charge more. First you need to know whether you have full or only basic protection as a tenant. See Chapter 2 for advice. If you are a fully protected regulated tenant, see Fair rents for regulated tenants, below. If you have only basic protection, you do not have any rights to get a rent registered.
- If your tenancy began on or after 15 January 1989 and the landlord tries to charge a rent higher than other open market rents in the area, you may be able to reduce this to a market rent (see page 109).
- Tenants may be eligible to claim money to help pay their rent through the housing benefit scheme (see page 120).

- Tenants have legal rights to challenge unreasonable service charges (see page 110).

Fair rents for regulated tenants

If you are a fully protected regulated tenant (see page 67) you have the right to get a fair rent fixed. This will usually mean that your tenancy began before 15 January 1989. Fair rents are fixed by the Rent Officer. Before deciding to apply to the Rent Officer it is very important to find out:

- Are you certain you are a regulated tenant? If you are not a regulated tenant, the Rent Officer cannot help you and, worse, any attempt to get your rent reduced could lead to you being evicted by the landlord. If you are in any doubt, seek advice. If you are a regulated tenant, the landlord cannot evict you because you go to the Rent Officer.

- What rents has the Rent Officer fixed on similar properties? The Rent Officer will look at rents fixed on similar properties when deciding what your rent should be. These other rents are known as comparables. The Rent Officer must also look at market rents being charged on similar properties in the area. The Rent Officer can put the rent up as well as down, so it is important to check on other rents before applying. Rent Officers keep a register of rents that is open for public inspection at their offices. Try to find a number of rent registrations on properties that are as close as possible to your home in terms of neighbourhood, size, amenities, floor level and facilities. Look at the most recent registrations because rents are always increasing. If comparable rents registered recently are lower than yours, it is probably worth applying for a fair rent. Keep a note of the addresses and rents fixed on what seem to be similar properties, because these will be useful in presenting your case to the Rent Officer. If you discover a fair rent has already been registered on your home (even if it was before you moved in) and you have been paying more than this, then you can reclaim the extra amount you have been paying for up to two years after it was paid. If the landlord will not reimburse you, you can go to court to get your money back or deduct it from future rent payments.

Applying to the Rent Officer

If you decide to apply for a fair rent you should get a form from the Rent Officer. You will have to give details of the accommodation and the rent you think should be registered. It is best to get help filling in this form from an advice centre. A copy of this completed form will be sent to the landlord who will be asked to say what s/he thinks the rent should be. Similarly, if it is the landlord who makes the application then you will get a copy of it and a chance to state what you think the rent should be. You can also make a joint application with the landlord if you have agreed a rent, although the Rent Officer will still make an independent assessment and could fix a different rent.

Before fixing a rent, the Rent Officer will usually visit to inspect your home and either then, or at another date, hold a consultation with you and the landlord to hear both sides. This is an informal hearing and it is not usually necessary to be represented, although you can be if you wish. If the landlord is likely to argue that you are not a regulated tenant and therefore the Rent Officer cannot fix a fair rent, you should get legal advice and you may want to be represented by a solicitor at the hearing. Help is not available, however, to pay for the solicitor's fees for representing you at the hearing, although you may get free advice before the hearing (see page 181).

In deciding what is a fair rent, the Rent Officer must take account of all the circumstances and in particular the property's age, character, locality, state of repair and the quality and condition of any furniture provided. The Rent Officer is not allowed to take account of the personal circumstances of landlord or tenant, so there is no point in arguing that you cannot afford to pay the rent because of your level of income (if this is a problem, see page 120 on claiming housing benefit). The Rent Officer will disregard any improvements you have made (unless you had to do them under the terms of the tenancy agreement) and any damage or disrepair that is your fault. Before the Rent Officer comes, you should make a note of all the things that are inadequate about the property and the neighbourhood. If you do not have a list of furniture agreed with the landlord, you should point out to the Rent Officer everything that belongs to you and not the landlord.

The Rent Officer also has to disregard any scarcity value of the property. If your home is in an area where there is a shortage of places to rent, rents that have not been fixed by the Rent Officer will be pushed up because of the large number of people chasing each home. The Rent Officer has to disregard this factor and fix a rent as if there were no shortage of homes in the area.

You should, within a few weeks of the Rent Officer's visit and consultation, receive written notice of the rent registered. This is the fair rent that will remain in force for a two-year period. If the rent has been reduced, this amount is the most the landlord can charge; it is payable from the date of registration, even if your tenancy agreement states that a higher rent is payable. If the rent has been increased, then the landlord may not be able to claim the full increase straight away. There are two reasons for this:

- If you have a fixed-term tenancy (see page 70) that has not yet expired and the amount of rent agreed is less than the fair rent that has been registered, then the landlord cannot make any increase until the fixed-term agreement does run out, unless the tenancy agreement states that s/he can do so.
- Before the landlord can make the increase, s/he must give a notice of increase in the proper form laid down by law.
- The increase is limited to a maximum of 7.5 per cent above the rate of inflation on the first re-registration and five per cent above inflation after that.

Once the rent has been fixed the landlord cannot make any further increases for at least two years except for any increases in variable service charges (see page 110). However, if the property has been greatly improved by the landlord then s/he can apply for a higher rent before the two years are up. But the rent cannot be increased because of improvements made by the tenant.

If the property has seriously deteriorated you could apply for a reduction in the rent. The only other circumstance in which a re-registration could be made in less than two years is where the landlord and tenant apply jointly for a new rent.

If either you or the landlord are dissatisfied with the fair rent that has been registered, you can appeal to the Rent Assessment Committee. This appeal normally has to be made within 28 days. In a high proportion of cases Rent Assessment Committees increase the rent to a higher level than that fixed by the Rent Officer, so it is inadvisable to appeal unless you are very confident the Rent Officer has made a mistake. Always seek advice before deciding to appeal.

Rents for assured tenants

If you have an assured tenancy (see page 58) then your landlord can charge a market rent, so there is little that you can do to reduce it. However, the landlord can only increase the rent once a year unless:

- the tenancy is for a fixed term (see page 70 for an explanation of this)
- the tenancy agreement states that the rent can be increased at an earlier date.

If neither of these conditions apply, then the landlord may serve a notice on you stating that a new rent will apply no earlier than one year after the tenancy began, plus a minimum period after the notice has been served. This minimum period must be at least a month if the rent is paid monthly or more often. If the rent is paid less frequently, then the notice period must be equal to the period for which rent is paid. In the unlikely event of rent only being paid yearly, then the period of notice is six months. The landlord can only serve such a notice once a year.

If you do not agree with the rent increase proposed by the landlord, you can apply to the local Rent Assessment Committee for a rent to be fixed. They will fix a rent that they think the landlord could get on the open market, disregarding any increase in value brought about by the tenants' own improvements to the property, or any decrease in value brought about by the tenant breaking the tenancy agreement. The rent they fix will not include service charges. Since the Rent Assessment Committee will fix the rent at a market level, there is likely to be little benefit in applying to them, unless you are certain that the landlord will not be able to evict you (see page 58) and the landlord is trying to exploit your wish to stay in your home by demanding a higher rent than s/he could otherwise get on the open market.

Rents for assured shorthold tenants

If you have an assured shorthold tenancy (see page 65), then the landlord is entitled to charge a market rent on the property and there is likely to be little you can do to reduce it. If, however, you believe that the rent is significantly higher than those charged for similar properties on the open market in the same area, then you can apply to the local Rent Assessment Committee who will decide what a market rent should be. You can only apply within six months of the start of the original tenancy. They will, however, only fix the rent if there is a sufficient number of similar lettings in the area for them to make a decision. This is unlikely to be of much help to you, unless from the beginning of the tenancy you were paying a much higher rent than the landlord could otherwise have gained on the open market and you do not mind increasing the likelihood of losing the tenancy when the shorthold agreement comes to an end.

Service charges in flats for private and housing association tenants and owner-occupiers with long leases

Private and housing association tenants and owners of long leases of flats (leaseholders) often have to pay a service charge to cover repairs to the block and provision of common services such as cleaning. There are additional rights for tenants' and residents' associations (see page 113).

If you are a tenant who is fully protected by the Rent Act 1977 (see page 67), or a housing association tenant whose tenancy began before 15 January 1989, and you have a fair rent fixed by the Rent Officer (see page 106) then check whether the Rent Officer has included in that fair rent the cost of services. If the cost of services is not included, or if you do not have a fair rent registered, or you are an owner-occupier with a long lease, then the amount of service charge the landlord can recover from you is controlled by law. Before any major repair work is carried out, you have a right to be consulted over the nature and cost of the work. You have a right to information from the landlord on how service charges are made up and a right to challenge unreasonable charges.

The right to be consulted and to challenge works before they begin

If the landlord wants to carry out building work, you have a right to be consulted in advance if it is likely to cost more than a certain amount, known as the prescribed amount. At present the prescribed amount is £100 a year per leasehold or tenancy for regular maintenance contracts, or £250 for one-off costs. The landlord must get at least two estimates for the work, at least one of them from a firm unconnected with the landlord. S/he must then give all the tenants and leaseholders who might have to pay the cost a notice describing the work to be done and copies of the estimates. The notice must give an address to which comments can be sent and a closing date for these comments. At least 30 days must be allowed for comments, unless the work is urgent. As an alternative to sending the separate notices to the tenants and leaseholders, the landlord can display copies in a prominent place in the building.

If the work is of a kind that your lease states the landlord can carry out, then you cannot usually prevent it from being done. However, if your lease does not authorise the landlord to carry out that kind of work, then you cannot be charged for it.

If you think the estimates are too expensive, you can get your own estimate and send it to the landlord. If the landlord does not consult you in advance, or does not give you the correct period in which to comment, then you could take the landlord to the Leasehold Valuation Tribunal (for more information about the Tribunal, visit www.rpts.gov.uk). If they find in your favour, the landlord will not normally be able to charge any more than the prescribed amount (ie, £100 a year for regular maintenance contracts, or £250 for one-off costs). Alternatively, you could simply pay only the prescribed amount and then it is up to the landlord to take action to try to recover the excess amount. However, if the landlord cannot go through the proper consultation procedures for good reason (for example, the work has to be carried out in an emergency) you may still have to pay your full share of the cost.

The landlord must hold service charges in a separate account.

The right to information on service charges

Landlords must provide a statement of service costs and charges at least annually, certified by an accountant. You have a right to a summary of what the landlord has spent to make up your service charge. You are entitled to ask for this for any one year, which may be the landlord's accounting year or the past 12 months. Once you have made your request in writing, the landlord must provide you with a summary of costs within one month, or six months of the end of the period covered by the summary, whichever is the later. If the summary does not give you enough information, you have a right to inspect the landlord's accounts and receipts.

If you do not know how to contact your landlord, you can give a written request to the person who collects the rent who must then send it to the landlord. If your landlord refuses to provide this information the local council can prosecute him/her.

The right to challenge unreasonable charges

If you think you should not have to pay a particular service charge, or if you think it is too high, tell your landlord or the agent. If you cannot reach agreement with the landlord you have two possible courses of action. You could take the landlord to the Leasehold Valuation Tribunal, which will decide whether you have to pay and if so, how much. Alternatively you could pay the amount you think is reasonable and then the landlord will have to take you to court if s/he disagrees.

The landlord can only charge in advance for services if this is allowed for in your lease and then can only make reasonable advance charges. Unreasonable charges can be challenged in the Leasehold Valuation Tribunal. If the work turns out to cost less than the advance payment, the landlord must repay the difference, or deduct that amount from future service charges. The landlord cannot charge for costs incurred more than 18 months before a demand for payment, unless s/he has informed you within 18 months that the costs had been incurred and that a service charge demand would follow.

Action through a tenants' or residents' association

Challenging service charges can be difficult for individual tenants and leaseholders. You could be much more effective by getting together with others to form a tenants' or residents' association, or joining one if it already exists. Associations with a sufficient number of members have a right to be recognised by the landlord.

Recognised associations have the same legal rights as individual tenants and leaseholders and some additional rights. They also have a better chance of being able to enforce these rights by acting together.

A recognised association can serve a notice on the landlord requiring them to provide details of managing agents and can comment on their brief and performance. Once such a notice has been served, the landlord must inform the tenants' and leaseholders' association of any proposal to change the managing agent, inform the association at least once every five years of any changes since the last notice, and invite comments on the agents and on whether they should be retained. The landlord must take notice of any comments made by the association about managing agents. The association can apply to the Leasehold Valuation Tribunal to appoint a managing agent if the landlord is failing to manage the building properly.

A recognised association can also challenge major works by the landlord before they have begun and appoint a qualified surveyor, at its own expense, to advise it on the landlord's proposed works.

If the landlord refuses to give written notice of recognition to your association, you can apply to the local Rent Assessment Panel (the address is in the telephone directory) for a certificate of recognition. There are no formal rules on which associations should be given recognition, but government guidelines suggest normally 60 per cent of tenants and leaseholders of flats in the block should belong to the association, although in some circumstances more than one association might be recognised. The Rent Assessment Panel can advise you on what you need to do to gain a certificate of recognition.

Insurance

Tenants and leaseholders can require their landlord to provide details of the insurance policy on their building. The landlord must provide a copy of the policy, or a summary of it, within 21 days. Within six months of receiving these details, tenants and leaseholders can require the landlord to allow them to inspect the full policy and details of payments. You can challenge unreasonable insurance policies in the Leasehold Valuation Tribunal, if the cost is paid by the tenants or leaseholders.

Ground rent

Most long leaseholders have to pay a ground rent to the landlord. This is only payable if the landlord has given you written notice in the proper form at least 30 days (and not more than 60 days) before the payment is due.

Council tenants

Rents

Local councils fix their own rents. The rents are supposed to be reasonable, but this leaves a very wide scope and it is extremely unlikely that a council's rent levels would be successfully challenged in the courts. Council tenants, like other tenants, can claim housing benefit to meet the cost of rent (see page 120).

Rent arrears

If you have difficulty in paying the rent and get into arrears, you could risk losing your home. If you have money problems, contact the local council immediately and explain why. In addition, seek independent advice to see whether you:

- Can get help with paying the rent by claiming housing benefit. If you are already getting housing benefit, check whether you are receiving the right amount (see page 120).

- Are entitled to other welfare benefits. There are a large number of benefits available, whether you are working or not. (See Useful publications on pages 191–192.)

If you have money problems, discuss them with the housing department as soon as possible. If the council takes you to court to evict you for rent arrears it may still be possible to save your home. Try to work out how you can pay off the arrears over a period of time, but make sure that any agreement you reach with the council is one that you can afford to keep.

If you have problems over paying the rent, or if you or your partner have run up rent arrears, the sooner you get advice the more chance you will have of saving your home.

Do not stop paying the rent because the council is failing to do repairs. Instead, see page 142 on how to force it to do the repairs.

Distraint' or 'distress' for rent arrears

Some councils resort to an ancient legal right that enables them to seize people's possessions and sell them to pay off debts such as rent arrears without even getting a court order. This is known as 'distraint' or 'distress'. However, the council may break the law if it fails to seize the goods in the correct manner. If you are threatened with this, seek advice immediately.

Housing association tenants

Rents

Rents for housing association tenants depend on whether the tenancy began before or after 15 January 1989. Tenancies that began before that date have fair rents fixed in the same way as regulated private tenants (see page 106). The housing association will automatically apply for a fair rent to be fixed, so there is no need for the tenant to take any action. Because housing associations are non-profit-making bodies, they do not have the same incentive as private landlords to try to increase tenants' rents, but you can still make any representations you wish to the Rent Officer. Tenancies that began on or after 15 January 1989 are assured tenancies with very little legal control over rent levels (see page 109). Help with paying the rent is available through the housing benefit scheme run by the local council (see page 120).

Rent arrears

Housing association tenants with difficulties in paying their rent are in much the same position as council tenants (see page 115). However, unlike councils, housing associations are not able to use the procedure of distraint to seize people's possessions without going to court first. As a result, its use is virtually unknown by non-council landlords.

Homeowners

Choosing the right mortgage

Mortgage costs can vary widely depending on the type of loan you have and the type of lender you borrow from. See page 35 for advice on the best value in mortgages.

If you are eligible for Income Support, Jobseeker's Allowance (JSA) or Pension Credit

If you are eligible for one of the above benefits you might also qualify for Income Support Mortgage Interest (ISMI). If you do qualify, the Benefits Agency will pay mortgage interest payments. They will usually only pay the interest on the loan taken out to buy the home, but they can also pay interest on a loan taken out for major repairs or improvements. The payment is based on a standard average interest rate, which might be lower than you are actually paying. They will not repay the capital part of the mortgage loan or insurance premiums for an endowment mortgage.

If you and your partner are aged over 60, you will receive help immediately. If you are under 60 and you took out your mortgage on or after 2 October 1995, you will not normally receive any benefit for the first 39 weeks. But you might be able to get payments sooner if:

- your mortgage started before 2 October 1995, or your mortgage replaces one on the same property taken out before that date
- you are a carer and the person you look after is eligible for certain benefits
- you are a single parent whose partner has died or left
- you are awaiting trial or sentence for a criminal offence
- your mortgage protection insurance won't pay out because of a medical condition you already had when you took out the mortgage.

If one of these apply you will normally have to wait for eight weeks before receiving any benefit, and then you will only receive half of your mortgage interest payments for the next 18 weeks of your claim, and all of the interest after 26 weeks. However, if you take up a job but then lose it again within a year, you will not have to wait another nine months for benefits. Help with mortgage payments will continue for a further four weeks after you take up work.

Other housing costs that can be covered by JSA and Income Support include:

– an allowance for repairs and insurance

– water rates

– ground rent if you are a long leaseholder

– some other service and maintenance charges for long leaseholders.

Homeowners on low incomes, whether they are working or not, can also claim help in paying the council tax from the local council (see below). The Jobcentre Plus should also notify the local council that you are entitled to receive benefit to help pay your council tax (see page 129).

Cutting mortgage costs

There are a number of ways you can consider reducing your mortgage costs. The options available to you depend on the number and type of mortgages you have. See page 35 for a description of the different types of mortgage.

Changing your mortgage

You might be able to save money by swapping to another mortgage lender. Check what deals are available (see Getting a mortgage loan, page 32), but also check what added costs are involved, for example, you might have to pay for legal expenses, a new valuation and application fees, which could add hundreds of pounds to the cost, although some lenders will pay these costs for you. When you have found the best deal, you could try going back to your current mortgage lender and asking if they can match it, because they may have special deals that they do not normally offer to existing customers.

If you have a capital repayment mortgage

If you only have one loan and it is a capital repayment mortgage, you can ask your lender to accept payment of interest only and to allow you to put off paying back any capital. You may particularly need to consider this if you are getting JSA or Income Support, because the Jobcentre Plus will only pay the interest part of a mortgage. If this is not possible you could, as an alternative, ask your lender to extend the period of the mortgage (for example, from 20 to 25 years), because this will reduce your payments.

If you have an endowment or interest-only mortgage

If you have only one loan and if it is an endowment or interest-only mortgage you could consider changing to a capital repayment mortgage because this is often cheaper. You will need to get your lender to agree to this.

You could also ask your lender to agree to let you pay interest only on the loan and to stop paying the insurance policy premiums that go towards paying off the capital. Again, this will be particularly important if you are getting JSA or Income Support, because the Jobcentre Plus will only pay for interest charges. However, many insurance policies are automatically cancelled if a certain number of premiums are not paid (for example six months' premiums), so your lender may only agree to this for a very short period.

If you have two or more mortgages

If you have more than one mortgage and are paying higher interest on one or more of them, you can try to rearrange all your borrowing on the cheapest basis. This will probably mean an ordinary capital repayment mortgage over a long period. If you have your first mortgage with a building society or major bank, ask them for help with a remortgage in this way. Alternatively, ask your local council for help with a remortgage if:

- your first mortgage is with that council

- your first mortgage is with a finance company or fringe bank

- your building society refuses to offer a remortgage, or you are in danger of losing your home.

Be careful if going to a finance company or fringe bank for a remortgage as they may charge high interest rates.

Mortgage arrears

If you have problems keeping up with your mortgage payments and get into arrears, your lender could eventually evict you and sell the property to recover its loan.

But even if you have got into arrears, there are many things you can do. Seek advice immediately and check:

- Can you reduce your mortgage costs? (see page 35)

- Can you get extra help with paying the mortgage and other costs? (see page 117)

- Are you getting all the welfare benefits to which you are entitled? There are a large number of benefits available, whether you are working or not.

- Could you claim a grant from the local authority to help with repairs or improvements? (see page 147)

If you have difficulty keeping up payments, contact your lender immediately and explain your difficulties. There are many ways of keeping your home – seek advice from an independent advice agency.

Housing benefit, local housing allowance and council tax benefit

Housing benefit is the name of the government scheme for helping people meet the cost of their rent. You can also get help with paying the council tax, by claiming council tax benefit. Details of this can be found on page 129. In a few areas a new local housing allowance (LHA) is paid instead of housing benefit for most private tenants. Your council will tell you if you are in one of those areas.

From April 2008, LHA will be extended to all areas for new customers and for exisiting customers when they have a break in their claim of at least one week. LHA is a flat rate allowance based on the size of your household and the area you live in, so it could be higher or lower than the actual rent you pay.

Local housing allowance aims to make the system simpler, because you will receive a flat rate amount, based on:

* average rents in your area
* the number of people in your household
* how much you can afford to pay towards your rent.

If the rent you pay is cheaper than average for similar-sized properties in the area, you can keep any extra local housing allowance that you receive, up to a maximum of £15 a week. If however your rent is above average, you will have to pay the difference, or negotiate a lower rent, or move to cheaper accommodation.

How local housing allowance is calculated

Local housing allowance is calculated by looking at how much you can pay towards your rent. But instead of taking this amount away from your maximum rent, it will normally be taken away from a standard local rent. The council can tell you what the standard local rents for your area are.

The council will normally work out how many bedrooms your household needs. This will depend on how many people live with you. The council will work out how much rent landlords in the area normally charge for similar-sized properties and deduct the amount it thinks you can afford to pay towards your rent.

If you are single and younger than 25, local housing allowance will normally only cover the average cost of a single room in a shared house in your area. This is the case, even if you rent a house or flat on your own. However, there are exceptions. This rule may not apply if:

- you live with a non-dependant (for example, in a flat share)
- you have children
- you live in a certain type of hostel
- you are living with a spouse, civil partner or partner
- you are under 22 and have spent time in care since the age of 16
- you are severely disabled
- you rent from the council or a housing association.

If you could afford the rent when you moved in and you have not claimed housing benefit in the past year, this restriction will not apply for the first 13 weeks.

Care leavers
If you've left care and you're still under 18, you probably won't be able to claim housing benefit or local housing allowance, but you will be entitled to financial support from social services. Once you reach 18 you can claim housing benefit or local housing allowance, provided you meet all the usual criteria.

Students
Most full-time students are not entitled to housing benefit or local housing allowance, but there are some exceptions. You may be entitled if:

- you are receiving a state pension
- you are on a part-time course
- you are getting Income Support or income-based Jobseeker's allowance

- you have a recognised disability
- you are responsible for children
- you are under 20 and someone is getting child benefit for you
- you are under 19 and taking a non-higher education course, such as A-levels
- you leave your course temporarily, because of illness or caring responsibilities.

If none of these applies to you, you're probably not entitled to help. The rules are complicated, and may affect the entitlement of people you live with (for example, a partner), so get advice. Your university or college welfare service should have specialist knowledge about claiming benefits as a student and can check your eligibility.

Housing benefit

The housing benefit scheme is extremely complicated. This section explains its main features, but does not cover all the details. If you have further questions get advice and also see Useful publications on pages 190–191 for more detailed guides available from Shelter.

Tenants and licensees are eligible for housing benefit for accommodation that they occupy as their home. This includes people living in hostels, bed and breakfast hotels and mobile homes, as well as ordinary tenancies. Around one in three households in Britain qualifies for housing benefit, which is usually paid by the local council. Private and housing association tenants can claim a rent allowance; council tenants can claim a rent rebate. All types of occupiers, tenants and homeowners can also claim council tax benefit for help with paying council tax.

People aged under 25 can only claim for the cost of a bedsit, not for self-contained accommodation, unless

- their claim dates back to before 2 January 1996
- they are part of a couple

- they have the care of children
- they are council or housing association tenants
- they are under 22 and have been previously housed by social services
- they have severe disabilities.

Your benefit will not necessarily be based on the full rent if the cost of your home is:

- above what the market rent would be
- above the average market rent (known as the local reference rent) for properties of a similar size in your area
- judged to be too big for your needs.

If your benefit has been reduced, you might be able to get an additional discretionary housing payment from the council. Contact them directly for information, and seek advice if you are refused.

Charges for most services such as caretaking, communal rooms and warden services for older people or people with disabilities, will generally be included too, provided you have to pay the charge as a condition of your tenancy. But payments for meals and for amenities such as heat and light are not included.

The way to claim depends on whether or not you are eligible for Jobseeker's Allowance (JSA) or Income Support from the Jobcentre Plus. If you are receiving JSA or Income Support (or think you may be eligible to receive it), see the section below. If you are not eligible for JSA or Income Support, see People not on JSA or Income Support on page 125. General points affecting everybody who gets housing benefit are dealt with on page 126. The figures at the end of this section will help you to work out whether you are likely to qualify.

People on JSA or Income Support

If you qualify for JSA or Income Support, you should receive a housing benefit claim form along with your JSA or Income Support claim form from the Jobcentre Plus. The Jobcentre

Plus should then send your housing benefit form on to the local council. If you are a council tenant, the council will work out your benefit. If you are a private or housing association tenant, you will have to fill in an additional form giving details of your tenancy, the amount of rent and council tax you pay and the number of people living in your household. If you have a subtenant, you will also have to give details of any income received from the subtenant.

Some deductions may be made from your benefit. These are:

- If you have subtenants, lodgers or people who count as non-dependants (for example, children over 18 who have left school, or older relatives) living with you, there will be a deduction from your benefit to take account of the contribution these people are assumed to make to your housing costs.

- If you are a tenant and have to pay service charges for the provision of common services such as caretaking, communal rooms, or wardens for older people and people with disabilities, most of these charges are eligible for benefit. However, payments for personal services provided to you, such as laundry or meals, are not eligible for benefit and the cost of these is deducted before calculating your housing benefit.

- Water rates are not eligible for housing benefit.

- Heating and fuel charges are not covered by housing benefit.

People not on JSA or Income Support

People who work can also get housing benefit, provided they (or they and their partner) do not have savings of more than £16,000.

To claim housing benefit you have to fill out a form provided by the local council. To assess whether you are entitled to benefit, the council will need to know:

- Your income and that of your spouse or partner. This will normally be based on your last five weeks' net earnings, after tax, if you are paid weekly, or two months' net earnings, after tax, if you are paid monthly. You will probably be asked to produce pay slips or other proof of earnings. If you are self-employed, the assessment is made on your net profits after Income Tax and National Insurance. Income other than earnings, including pensions and state benefits such as Child Benefit and income from investments, is taken into account. But certain amounts of income are disregarded. These are known as income disregards. All of them are deducted from your income before any calculation of benefit.

- How many people live in your home and whether they are related to you. Families and couples who live together are usually assessed together, but unrelated people sharing a home who are not married or living together should be assessed individually.
- The rent you pay.

Deductions may be made for non-dependants or subtenants in the same way as for people on JSA or Income Support (see above).

All claimants: how housing benefit is paid

The council should give you a written statement of how much benefit you are entitled to receive within 14 days of getting a completed application form from you, or from the Jobcentre Plus if you are getting JSA or Income Support. If for any reason your application form did not contain all the information needed to make the assessment, the council can ask you for the necessary extra information and then have a further 14 days within which it should tell you how much benefit you will receive.

For council tenants the amount of your rent rebate is deducted from the amount of rent you pay.

For private and housing association tenants the rent allowance is paid directly to you, usually by Giro or cheque, but you can ask for other arrangements if those do not suit. The council can decide to make this payment on a monthly or fortnightly basis, but you can insist on a fortnightly payment if you are getting a rent allowance of more than £2 a week. Your benefit should be paid to you, not to your landlord, but it can be paid directly to the landlord if you ask for, or agree, to it being paid in this way. If you are a tenant and you owe more than eight weeks' rent, the landlord can ask for your benefit to be paid directly to him/her.

How long housing benefit lasts

If you are on JSA or Income Support, then your housing benefit will continue as long as your entitlement to JSA or Income Support, but you will have to fill in a fresh claim form, usually each year. If you are a private or housing association tenant and your rent or rates go up, you should tell the council immediately, because you will probably be entitled to more benefit.

If you come off JSA or Income Support, you may still qualify for housing benefit, depending on your new level of income. Notify the council immediately of this or any other change in your circumstances that might affect your entitlement to benefit.

If you are not getting JSA or Income Support, but are getting housing benefit, then this benefit will be reassessed regularly. It will normally last for between six months and just over a year before being reassessed by the council.

If you are away from home

You can still get housing benefit if you are away from home for a while; for example, on holiday, looking for a job elsewhere, in hospital or in prison, providing you still have to pay rent and council tax on your home. Benefit can be paid for periods of up to one year's absence from home at the discretion of the local council, except in the case of prisoners who have been convicted and are serving a sentence of more than 13 weeks, who are not entitled to benefit.

Normally, you can only get benefit on one home. There are, however, two exceptions:

- If you are obliged to make payments for two homes at the same time (for example, because you are moving home) you may get housing benefit on both for a period of up to 28 days.

- If you have to make payments for two homes at the same time because you have left one through fear of violence, you may get housing benefit on both for up to 52 weeks.

Appealing against the assessment of housing benefit

If you think there has been a mistake in assessing your entitlement you have a right to appeal. If you are considering appealing, then get independent advice to help you do so. The procedure works as follows:

- If you do not agree with the council's assessment, you should ask if necessary for a fuller explanation showing how your claim was assessed. Write to the council and keep a copy of the letter. The council should send you a full written explanation within 14 days.

- If you are still not satisfied, write to the council explaining why. You must do this within one month and they should let you know, within two weeks and in writing, whether the original assessment is confirmed or altered.

- If you are still not satisfied, you can appeal to an independent tribunal. Your appeal must be made in writing, explaining why you disagree and where you think the council's decision is wrong. You must do this within one month of the council's review of its decision. You are entitled to attend and also to be accompanied or represented by someone else. If your appeal is successful, the decision is backdated to the date of your application.

If your appeal is unsuccessful and you still think the council is wrong, it may be possible to take the case to court or to complain to the Ombudsman (see page 169). If you are thinking of doing either of these things it is important that you get further independent advice as soon as possible. The case can only be taken to court if you consider that the review board has wrongly interpreted the law, or failed to take account of all the facts, or reached its decision unreasonably or in an improper manner.

Reducing your council tax and claiming council tax benefit

Council tax is collected by local councils to pay for local services. Almost all residents have to pay, including homeowners and tenants, and it is charged on individual homes. The tax is calculated by placing every property into one of eight bands, based on its market value on 1 April 1993. Some dwellings are exempt from the tax, including:

- halls of residence mainly occupied by students
- other properties where all the residents are students
- armed forces accommodation.

Empty properties are exempt where the former resident is:

- in prison or detention
- receiving care in a hospital, care home or nursing home
- living with someone else to provide them with care
- a student.

Empty properties are also exempt if:

- they have been repossessed by a mortgage lender
- they are reserved for a minister of religion.

Empty properties are exempt for six months if they are:

- substantially unfurnished, including new properties and those that have undergone major works
- owned or used by a charity.

The tax is normally paid by the person who lives in the accommodation. In some cases, mainly houses in multiple occupation, most hostels and residential care and nursing homes, the owners rather than the residents are liable to pay the tax. Where there is more than one owner, or joint tenants of a property, they are jointly liable to pay. There are four main ways of reducing your council tax bill:

- You are entitled to a 25 per cent discount if you live alone. People who are students, apprentices, trainees or severely mentally impaired are exempt, so someone may count as living alone if the only other people in the dwelling come into these categories.

- You are entitled to a 50 per cent discount if the property has been empty for more than six months, or is a second home.
- If the home has certain major adaptations for a person with disabilities, you can apply to the council for a reduction in the bill that will put it in the next valuation band down.
- People on low incomes who have less than £16,000 savings can apply for council tax benefit. If you claim JSA or Income Support, your Jobcentre Plus office should give you a claim form. Everyone else should apply to the local council.

Usually you can pay the tax in ten monthly instalments throughout the year. In a few areas council tenants can pay their tax at the same time as they pay their rent. If you live in a hostel, the landlord will tell you if you have to pay a contribution and will collect it with your rent.

People with no home

If you have nowhere to live, the Jobcentre Plus should pay you benefit and money for somewhere to stay. This could include:

- paying the cost of a hostel
- referring you to a project for homeless people.

People from abroad

There are certain groups of people who, because of their nationality or immigration status, may lose their right to stay in the country if they claim certain benefits. The rules governing this are complicated and if you are at all unsure of whether to claim benefit, seek advice immediately. If you do claim certain benefits when you are prohibited from claiming because of your nationality or immigration status, you may jeopardise your stay in the UK and risk deportation.

Improving conditions in your home: repairs, improvements and overcrowding

4

Private tenants and housing association tenants

In almost all cases, private and housing association landlords are legally responsible for repairs to the houses of their tenants. Tenants have a right to repairs under a number of different Acts of Parliament and also under common law. Your tenancy agreement may also set out your rights to get repairs done, although it cannot transfer to you any obligations to do repairs that are, in law, the landlord's responsibility. So you should always check on your other legal rights, in addition to looking at the tenancy agreement. The first part of this section gives an outline of these legal rights and the second part gives advice on how to enforce them.

Your rights to repairs

Whose responsibility?

Section 11 of the Landlord and Tenant Act 1985 sets down a comprehensive list of repairs that are always the landlord's responsibility. This covers almost all tenancies. The only exceptions are where:

- the tenancy began before 24 October 1961
- the lease you originally agreed was for a fixed term of more than seven years.

The law states that the landlord has to repair the structure, exterior and installations of the dwelling. This includes:

- repairs to the structure such as the roof, walls, floors and windows
- upkeep of the outside of the building, including gutters, pipes and drains
- repair of plumbing and sanitary conveniences such as baths, toilets, sinks and basins
- repair of installations such as electrical wiring, gas piping, fixed heaters and water heaters.

By law these are your landlord's responsibility, even if your tenancy agreement states that they are not. However, this does not require the landlord to rebuild/restore property destroyed by flood or fire.

Enforcing your rights to repair

The first step is to tell your landlord, or the person who collects your rent, what repairs need doing. If you do not know who your landlord is, you have a legal right to be given the name and address by the landlord's agent or the person who collects the rent. You may need proof that you have told your landlord what needs to be done, so it is important to put your request for repairs in writing and to keep a copy of the letter. Even if you made your first request by word of mouth, you should follow it up with a letter. If the landlord still does not do the repairs, there are different ways you can choose to enforce your rights:

- you can ask the local council to inspect the property and take action requiring the landlord to do the repairs
- you can take action yourself, which may include taking the landlord to court to get the repairs done and also to claim damages.

Often you can pursue more than one line of action at the same time. For example, you could notify the local authority and pursue your own action at the same time. You should not simply stop paying rent in an attempt to force the landlord to do repairs, because the landlord may start court action to evict you.

Although there are certain circumstances in which it is possible to get the work done yourself and to deduct the cost from the rent (see page 140), or to set the cost of repairs against any rent arrears, you should never do this without good legal advice and support, as it could result in you losing your home.

If you are a private tenant, you need to check whether or not you have protection from eviction. If you are not fully protected, any attempt to enforce your legal rights to repair could result in the landlord evicting you. If you think you may not be fully protected, seek advice before taking any legal action.

Local councils' powers and duties

Local councils have a wide range of legal powers and duties to require landlords to improve the condition of their property. These powers are set down in the Environmental Protection Act 1990 and the Housing Act 2004. The next section describes the powers under the Environmental Protection Act and the following section the powers under the Housing Act.

Local councils can and should, if necessary, use powers under both Acts at the same time. As a general rule, their powers under the Housing Act are more comprehensive than under the Environmental Protection Act.

Local councils' powers under the Environmental Protection Act

Councils can use these powers when the property is in such a bad state as to be a statutory nuisance. This is defined as 'any premises in such a state as to be prejudicial to health or a nuisance'. This usually means that the fault is likely to affect your health. Examples of some of the types of fault covered by this are:

- dampness
- leaking roof
- rotten floorboards
- piles of rubbish
- rotten window frames.

If the council is satisfied that there is such a statutory nuisance, it must serve a notice known as an Abatement Notice on the person responsible. This orders the repairs to be done and gives a time by which the work must be finished. If the time limit runs out and the repairs have not been done, the council may apply to the magistrates' court for an order against the landlord. The magistrate can order the landlord to do the repairs and may impose a fine. You could also make a separate application to be awarded compensation if you can show that you have suffered injury or your property has been damaged because the repairs were not done. If the landlord still does not do the repairs, s/he can be fined for every day that the work is not done after the notice has expired. Finally, the council can do the repairs in default and claim the cost from the landlord. However, the council does not have to take this final step if it does not wish to.

This can all take a very long time; nine months is not unusual. If there is an urgent need for repairs, for example if your roof is leaking and the ceiling is likely to collapse, the council can serve on the landlord a Nine Day Notice. This states that the council will do the work itself, giving at least nine days' notice. The landlord can notify the council within seven days that s/he will do the repairs, but the council can still step in if the repairs are not started within a reasonable time. However, even this emergency procedure can take a long time.

There are special arrangements to clear blocked drains and toilets within two days. The council can serve a notice on the landlord giving 48 hours for them to be unblocked. If they are not, the council can do the work and charge the landlord the costs.

There are two main problems with using Environmental Protection Act powers. First, many of the procedures are very lengthy and time-consuming for the local council. Many councils do not use the powers as fully as they could. This can mean that there are long delays, often of many months, or even that the work is not done at all. The second problem is that, under the Act, all the landlord has to do is to stop the immediate problem and the likelihood of it recurring. This could mean, for example, merely replacing damp plaster, rather than installing a damp-proof course. Underlying defects may be ignored. So, for example, if there is a leaking roof this may just be patched up rather than properly repaired. However, if the problem is likely to return, the local council can serve another notice that can order the landlord to do a better job to prevent the problem recurring.

Local council powers and duties under the Housing Act 2004

The Housing Act 2004 has introduced a new system for assessing housing conditions. The system is based on the principle that any residential premises should provide 'a safe and healthy environment for any potential occupier or visitor'. The system is called the Housing Health and Safety Rating System, and it includes a complex calculation based on a wide range of different hazards and the degree of risk to the most vulnerable occupant of the property. The hazards include all types of defect that might present a risk, even small ones such as a loose floorboard that someone might trip over. The system calculates the seriousness of the hazards in a dwelling by reference to the likelihood of the harm occurring and the severity of the harm if it were to occur. The highest risks and most dangerous hazards are known as Category 1 and lesser dangers as Category 2.

The local authority must inspect the property if it believes it is necessary to establish whether a hazard exists, or if an official complaint is made by a local Justice of the Peace or a parish or community council.

If there is a Category 1 hazard the local authority has a duty to take the best course of action available to it to remedy the problem. The courses of action it can take are:

- Serving a hazard awareness notice. This notifies the person responsible that a hazard exists and the actions the authority considers it would be practicable to take to remedy it.
- Declaring a clearance area, if other buildings in the area are also harmful to health or safety.

- Serving an improvement notice. This sets out what remedial action must be taken and the time allowed for it. If there is more than one problem it can give different deadlines for each one. The minimum time limit for starting the work is 28 days. The authority can suspend an improvement notice, for example until the current occupier moves out.

- Making a prohibition order. This may prevent someone from living in all or part of the building. It can apply to all people or only certain groups, for example people over the age of 65 or under the age of five. If there is an imminent risk of serious harm the authority can make an emergency prohibition order, which takes effect immediately.

- Taking emergency remedial action. If there is an imminent risk of serious harm, the authority can itself take emergency action to remedy the problem and recover its expenses.

- Making a demolition order.

If there is a Category 2 hazard the local authority has a power (but not a duty) to take any of the above actions, except the emergency actions.

Getting the council to require your landlord to do repairs

The legal powers and duties of local councils to require landlords to do repairs and remedy other problems with the condition of your home are described above. If your landlord is failing to do repairs or remedy other problems with the condition, you should contact the council's environmental health department and ask for an officer to visit your home. It is best to telephone before 10am or after 4pm, because the officers are usually out visiting between those times. The Environmental Health Officer should arrange a date for a visit. Try to get the name of the person who is dealing with your case, because you may need to contact him/her again. If there are other tenants in the house tell them about the visit, because the Environmental Health Officer may want to see the rest of the house.

Before the visit, it is a good idea to make a list of all the problems you want to complain about and to give it to the officer. Keep a copy for yourself. Get the name of the officer who calls and ask to be kept informed about what the landlord will be required to do and how long s/he will be given to do it. Ask for a copy of any notices the council sends to the landlord. Environmental health departments do not always use all the powers available to them and are sometimes very slow to act. If the council is not using all its powers, is failing in its duties or is taking a long time to act, there are a number of actions you can take:

- Your local councillor or a local advice or law centre may be able to contact the council on your behalf.

- If they still fail to act you could complain to the Local Government Ombudsman or the Local Government Monitoring Officer (see page 169).

Taking action yourself against the landlord

You can take your landlord to court directly, without the help of the local council. If you are considering doing this, always get advice first as there is a range of different types of action you can take. You may be able to get someone from an advice or law centre to represent you free of charge, or you may get help with the costs (see page 184). There are advantages and disadvantages to taking action yourself. The main advantages are:

- **Time**: if you can get an early court hearing this can be quicker than getting the council to serve notices. Many cases do not reach court because the landlord does the repairs before the hearing. But courts in some areas are very busy and delays can be quite long.

- **Money**: in certain actions you can claim for damages to property or decorations and for inconvenience to yourself.

The main disadvantages are:

- **Costs**: you may have to pay solicitors' fees and court costs, though depending on your income and the action you are taking you may be entitled to public funding (formerly known as legal aid). If you get help with the costs, some may be taken out of any compensation you get. For claims under £5,000 in value, you can use the small claims procedure. This limit is reduced to £1,000 if work is needed on your home and the value of any other claims does not exceed £1,000.

- **Limitations**: you cannot be sure the court will grant you everything you ask for.
- **Proof**: you and your advisers will be responsible for providing proof of the problem and of how it is affecting you. This may mean getting a surveyor or Environmental Health Officer to provide an independent report. In addition, you may need to take photographs of the disrepair and prove damage to your belongings if you wish to claim compensation. You have a right to summon witnesses, for example the local council's Environmental Health Officer, and to obtain relevant documents from the landlord.

If you decide to take action yourself your main rights are set out in:

- section 11 of the Landlord and Tenant Act 1985
- section 82 of the Environmental Protection Act 1990
- the Defective Premises Act 1972
- your tenancy agreement.

If your landlord fails to repair the structure or fixtures: section 11 of the Landlord and Tenant Act 1985

Section 11 sets out the legal responsibilities of landlords to keep the structure and installations of the building repaired (see page 131). If your landlord fails to do this you can apply to the county court for:

- an order that the work is done
- damages for the cost of any loss you have suffered and for your inconvenience.

In order to take action, ensure that your landlord has been given reasonable notice that the repairs are needed. Put your request in writing and keep a copy. What is a reasonable time will depend on all the circumstances, including the scale of the work needed and the effect the disrepair is having on you. If your landlord does not do the work, then it is advisable to get a solicitor or adviser to help and to represent you. Many cases are settled before the court hearing, but you may have to go to court. The court will take into account whether the repairs can be done at reasonable expense bearing in mind the age, character, locality and potential lifespan of the building and the neighbourhood. If you live in an old house in a run-down area, the court will not expect such a high standard of repair as for other areas or for more modern homes.

The court can decide whether or not to order the repairs to be done, but must, if the case is proved, award damages. The level of damages will depend, among other things, on the nature of the disrepair, the time you have put up with it, its effect on you and the amount of rent you pay.

Getting repairs done: section 82 of the Environmental Protection Act 1990

Section 82 enables you to take the landlord to court yourself, if the disrepair counts as a statutory nuisance (see page 133 for the definition of this). You should seek advice before taking any action. If you decide to go ahead, then you or your legal representative will need to take out a summons in the magistrates' court giving details of the problem. The summons will set a date for a court hearing where both sides can put their case. The magistrate may also want to visit your home. If the court decides there is a statutory nuisance then it must order the landlord to end the nuisance by doing the repairs within a certain time. This is known as a 'nuisance order'. It may also fine the landlord, and grant you compensation (if you have asked for it), and costs. If the work is not completed within the time ordered, you can go back to court for a further order, fines and compensation.

Other legal actions

In addition to these actions, if may be possible to:

- get a court order for repairs that are specified as being the landlord's responsibility in the tenancy agreement
- sue the landlord for damages for any negligence on his/her part.

Seek advice before taking either of these actions.

Defective Premises Act 1972

Under section 4 of the Defective Premises Act 1972, a landlord who has an obligation to carry out repairs, or who has a right to enter premises to carry out repairs, has a legal duty to prevent injury to people or damage to property arising from defects in the premises. This Act does not actually help directly in getting repairs done, but it does provide a way of getting compensation for personal injury or damage to property. The landlord's duty arises if the repair is the landlord's legal responsibility and they know of the defect or should have known of it. So even if the landlord did not actually know of the disrepair but should have known, you might be able to sue them for compensation. These rights cover not only tenants, but also licensees and visitors of the tenant or licensee of the premises.

Using the rent to pay for the repairs

A tenant has no right to simply withhold rent in protest at the landlord's failure to carry out repairs. Many tenants faced with a landlord unwilling to do repairs, particularly minor repairs, are reluctant to get the council involved or to threaten legal action. They may decide to do the repairs themselves and deduct the cost of the repairs from the rent. This course of action is risky, especially if you have little security of tenure, but the common-law right of tenants to do the repairs themselves has been confirmed by the courts in recent years.

If you wish to use this self-help remedy, you should follow the steps listed below carefully.

- Give notice in writing to your landlord of the repairs that need doing, keeping a copy of your letter (and all subsequent letters). Work out exactly how many weeks' rent you will be withholding. Only rent can be deducted. You have to continue paying any other sums you owe the landlord, such as service charges.
- Obtain two or three estimates for the repairs from reputable builders.
- After a reasonable time has elapsed, write again, enclosing copies of the estimates, stating that the landlord is in breach

of his/her repairing obligations and that unless the work is done within a specified period (say two weeks) you will do the work yourself and deduct the cost from the rent.

* If there is no response, go ahead with the work. When you pay your contractor make sure you obtain proper receipts.

* Write to your landlord, explaining precisely how the rent deductions will be made to cover the cost of the work.

* Withhold rent until the cost of the repairs has been covered.

You may be entitled to withhold an extra amount to cover, for example, damage done to your property, or the distress and inconvenience suffered. You should provide the landlord with the documentary evidence you have, ask for reimbursement, and state that if s/he fails to pay you, you will have to recover this sum by deducting it from your rent. It is best to claim too little rather than too much when asking for additional compensation. This is because if the courts decide that you have withheld too much rent, they will order you to pay your landlord some back rent and you may be asked to pay your landlord's legal costs as well.

You should not run up arrears before doing the repairs, although some tenants decide to stop payment as a means of trying to force the landlord to do the repairs.

If your landlord decides to sue you or tries to evict you for rent arrears, you can 'set-off' the total cost of the work (plus additional compensation you are claiming) in defending the action against the rent arrears. You would need legal advice to do this. Taking this self-help remedy requires careful preparation. If you are thinking of using it, get advice first.

Doing improvements yourself

If you are a fully protected tenant and you haven't been given notice by your landlord that one of the mandatory Rent Act grounds for possession applies (see page 74), you have the same rights as public sector tenants to make improvements (see page 145). You have to get the written agreement of your landlord, but this cannot be unreasonably withheld. If you spend your own money on improvements, you do not have a right to claim it back from the landlord, even if you paid for work that the landlord could have been made to do. On the other hand, the landlord cannot normally put up the rent because of improvements you have made.

Council tenants

Council tenants have many of the same legal rights to repair as private tenants. However, there are two big differences. First, local councils cannot serve notices on themselves requiring work to be done, so council tenants cannot make use of the legal provisions that require the service of notices by Environmental Health Officers. However, councils have been encouraged by a government circular to introduce and publish arrangements whereby, if a council tenant calls in an Environmental Health Officer, the officer will notify the housing department of any defects that would, in the private sector, lead to notices being served under the Housing Act 1985. The housing department should then ensure that the necessary repairs are carried out within a reasonable time.

The second main difference between council and private tenants is that councils are democratically elected and publicly accountable. This means that you may be able to put public pressure on the council to do repairs.

Councils, like private landlords, have legal responsibility for the structure and fixtures of the building under section 11 of the Landlord and Tenant Act 1985 (see page 131 for more details of the items for which they are responsible). Councils are responsible for those items even if the tenancy agreement says that they are not. Responsibility for other items of repair will depend on what is set out in your tenancy agreement and the council should by law provide you with clear details of your rights to get repairs done.

If the repair is the council's responsibility, you should inform it as soon as possible and confirm your complaint in writing. It is important to keep a copy of the letter, because you may need evidence later on if there is any delay. You need to give the council reasonable time to do the repair. Councils must give guidelines to tenants on how long it will take to do particular jobs. Obviously some are more urgent than others. A broken sash cord may wait several weeks, but a toilet that is blocked and cannot be used should be repaired within 48 hours. Most councils have an emergency service for problems like this and if the repair is urgent you should ring the council directly.

If the repair is unreasonably delayed, contact the housing department again, confirming any telephone calls in writing. If you are still getting nowhere, then there are a number of things you can do to make the council do the repairs. You can:

- put extra pressure on the council, for example through your tenants' association or by contacting a local councillor
- take the council to court to force it to do repairs and perhaps pay you compensation
- in certain limited circumstances, get the work done yourself and deduct the cost from the rent, or claim reimbursement from the landlord.

You should never simply stop paying rent, because the council might then evict you for rent arrears, nor should you give up the tenancy. If you do either, you may find yourself homeless and the council may refuse you any further help (see page 14 on intentional homelessness). If you are in this position, seek advice immediately.

The best course of action will depend on your own circumstances. You can take legal action and put public pressure on the council. The following sections look in turn at the different courses of action.

Putting extra pressure on the council

Councils are publicly accountable through their elected councillors. This means that putting public pressure on the council may be a more effective method of getting repairs done than legal action. The first step is to contact your tenants' association to ask them if they can take up your complaint. If there is no tenants' association, you might consider getting together with other tenants to set one up. Tenants' associations can develop links with councillors and housing staff and can mount campaigns, so they can be more effective in taking up complaints than individuals, who are easier to ignore. Action through tenants' associations may be particularly important if the problem is one that affects a group of tenants, for example building faults on an estate.

You can also take up the complaint directly with your local councillor. They are elected to represent you and good councillors will always be willing to take up individual complaints. You can find out the names of the local councillors for your neighbourhood from the Town Hall or local council office. Many hold local advice sessions (or surgeries) when you can call and see them. The Town Hall will have details of these sessions. Ask your local councillor to take up the complaint on your behalf. This can often be enough to get action from the housing department.

In addition, if the problem is particularly bad, you could try getting a story in your local paper. No council likes bad publicity and local newspapers are always on the look-out for stories. Telephone your local paper and ask for the News Desk. If you have a tenants' association, ask for their help in gaining publicity.

If all else fails, you could complain to the Local Government Ombudsman. The Ombudsman investigates cases of management inefficiency and unreasonable delay by local councils. They publish a booklet that explains how to complain, entitled *Your Local Ombudsman*. You can find copies in advice centres or order one directly from the Ombudsman (see Useful contacts on page 195). The main drawbacks with the

Ombudsman are that they often take many months to investigate and reach a decision and that they cannot order a council to do anything, although councils will usually take their findings very seriously.

You can also complain to the council's Local Government Monitoring Officer who must prepare a report for the council if they think that the council is likely to contravene the law or cause maladministration. This report must be considered within 21 days of it being sent.

Taking action yourself

Environmental Health Officers cannot take their own councils to court. However, all those courses of action that can be taken directly by private tenants can also be taken by council tenants. These actions are:

- court action where the council has failed in its repairing obligations under section 11 of the Landlord and Tenant Act 1985 (see page 138)

- court action under section 82 of the Environmental Protection Act 1990 (see page 139)

- other actions for damages and to secure repairs that are the landlord's responsibility under the tenancy agreement (see page 139)

- using the rent to pay for repairs (see page 140).

If you are considering taking action, always seek independent advice first.

The 'right to repair'

Council tenants have a right for repairs to be carried out within a fixed time. If the landlord fails to do so, you can notify them that you want a different contractor to do the job. You are entitled to compensation if repairs are still not carried out within the agreed timescale. The maximum compensation that can be claimed is £50. You can get details of the scheme from your local council.

The right to make improvements to your home

You have the right to make improvements to your home, but you must get the landlord's written agreement first. If the landlord refuses permission, you can challenge this in the county court. It is the landlord's responsibility to prove that s/he is being reasonable. The landlord might, for example, argue that the work you propose would reduce the value or safety of the property. When landlords refuse permission they must give their reasons in writing. The landlord cannot put up the rent because of improvements you have made. There is a right to compensation for any improvements made with the written agreement of the landlord. This payment is made at the end of the tenancy, but can be offset against any rent arrears.

People in council temporary accommodation

The position of people in council temporary accommodation is more complicated than that of permanent council tenants. The most important thing to know is whether you are classed as a tenant or a licensee, because this will affect your rights.

Most people in council hostels, reception centres or other temporary accommodation are not tenants, but only licensees, who have fewer rights to repairs (see page 56 for more details on licensees). To find out if you are a tenant or a licensee, look at your rent book or other papers that the council gave you when you moved in. These will include either the words 'licensee' and 'licence agreement' or the words 'tenant' and 'tenancy agreement'.

If you are a tenant in temporary accommodation, you have almost the same rights as permanent tenants. However in some cases, the council is temporarily allowed to use properties that are in a poor condition, but are considered adequate for use until they are repaired or demolished (usually where the council has bought the property from a private owner).

If you are a licensee you have fewer rights. You can, however, use section 82 of the Environmental Protection Act 1990 (see page 139) and can sue for damages.

If you have been put in a privately owned bed and breakfast hotel or hostel by the council, you are not a council tenant or licensee. You do still, however, have legal rights that will depend on the type of letting you have. Seek advice.

Housing association tenants

Action through a tenants' association

Housing association tenants have all the same rights as tenants of private landlords to get repairs done but, because their landlords are publicly accountable and non-profit-making, they may be able to make swifter progress in getting repairs done by putting pressure on the landlord through a tenants' association.

The 'right to repair'

Housing association tenants now have a right to compensation if repairs are not carried out within a fixed timescale. The maximum compensation that can be claimed is £50. Details of the scheme are available from your housing association.

The right to make improvements to your home

Housing association tenants have similar rights to council tenants to make improvements to their homes (see pages 145–146).

Renovation grants and loans for private homes

There are special grants and loans available from local councils to help with the cost of improving run-down homes. Councils can set up their own schemes to help with the improvement of privately owned homes or to help people move to more suitable accommodation. These grants or loans are normally for bringing houses up to a decent standard – for example, doing essential repairs or improvements. Contact the council for details of your local scheme.

Disabled facilities grants

Disabled facilities grants are available to make the homes of people with disabilities more suitable for them to live in.

Anyone who is registered or who could be registered as disabled, or anyone who has such a person living in their home, can apply for a grant. You should contact the social services department of your local council if you are not sure whether you could be registered as disabled. Homeowners and tenants, including council, housing association and private tenants and people living in mobile homes can all apply, as long as you intend to continue occupying the property as your only, or main home.

Certain basic works qualify for mandatory grants, while a wide range of other works may qualify for discretionary grants. The council will advise you of your eligibility. The amount of grant you receive is calculated by a test of your financial resources.

Group repair

The council can also undertake schemes to repair the external fabric, for example the roofs, of groups of properties. It organises the works and meets at least some of the cost. You might also qualify for extra help, up to the full cost of your share of the work. The council can only go ahead with the agreement of the owners of all the properties in the scheme.

Grants for heating and insulation

There are grants available for heating improvements and insulation. If you are a homeowner or private tenant and in receipt of a means tested benefit (for example, housing benefit, council tax benefit, Jobseekers Allowance) you may be eligible for a grant of up to £2,700, or £4,000 if oil central heating is involved.

People who may be eligible include those aged 60 or over, those with a child under 16, or pregnant women in receipt of income-related benefits, or people in receipt of a disability benefit or premium.

The grants are managed for the Government by independent agencies – for further details see Warm Front in Useful contacts on page 199.

Overcrowding

The law on overcrowding affects both landlords and tenants. At the time of writing, the Government is consulting on introducing a new overcrowding standard. This section describes the current standards.

There are two different tests of overcrowding. If you fail either of these tests then you are statutorily overcrowded.

- **The Room Standard**: by this test, you are overcrowded if there are so many people in your home that two or more people aged ten or over of opposite sexes are forced to sleep in the same room. Couples living together as man and wife do not count; nor do children under ten. The living room, dining room, and even the kitchen may be counted if it is big enough to hold a bed.

- **The Space Standard**: the space standard gives the maximum number of people who may live in accommodation of a particular size. There are two different ways of assessing this. One is by how many people can be accommodated by reference to the number of rooms; the other by how many people can live in each room according to its size. You have to work out both ways and then take whichever is the lower number of people as the maximum number who are allowed to live there.

First, take the number of people living there: children between one and ten years old count as half a person and children under one year old do not count at all. Next, count up the number of rooms. A kitchen can count as a living room, but rooms of less than 50 square feet do not count. The following table shows the maximum number of people allowed for each number of rooms:

Number of rooms	Number of people allowed
1	2
2	3
3	5
4	7½
5	10
Each extra room	2 extra people

The other test is based on the size of rooms and shows the number of people (calculated in the same way as before) allowed in each room size. The following table shows the number of people allowed in each size of room:

Size of room	Number of people allowed
Less than 50 square feet	0
50–69 square feet	½
70–89 square feet	1
90–109 square feet	1½
110 square feet and more	2

If you fail either of these space standard tests, or if you fail the room standard test, then you are, by law, overcrowded. In certain circumstances, overcrowding may be permitted. First, the tenant (but not the landlord) can apply to the local council for a licence for not more than a year at a time to allow overcrowding. Second, if the overcrowding is caused by family members staying with you temporarily, this does not count as illegal overcrowding. Third, the overcrowding may have occurred by natural growth, in other words a child reaches the age where it counts as an extra half or one person, thereby taking the family over the permitted number of people. If this occurs and you apply to the local council for alternative accommodation before any prosecution, the overcrowding is not considered illegal. If, however, the local council offers you suitable alternative accommodation and you turn it down, the overcrowding will be illegal. If you are the cause of illegal overcrowding, the landlord can go to court to evict you.

Overcrowding in houses in multiple occupation

Councils have wider discretion in houses in multiple occupation (HMOs) than in other housing to decide what is overcrowding, and are not limited to the definitions of illegal overcrowding that apply to other properties (see page 149). Overcrowding in licensed HMOs will be dealt with by the conditions attached to the licence. For other HMOs, the local authority will be able to serve notices to limit the number of people who can live in them.

Extra controls on some private rented homes

There is a new scheme for licensing some private rented homes. Most licensed properties are likely to be HMOs (see page 152). But local authorities are also able to introduce selective licensing schemes in areas of low demand for private rented housing or where there is antisocial behaviour. The requirements on landlords included in licences in these areas are similar to those for HMOs including the condition of the accommodation and the management standards (see page 152).

Local authorities are also able to apply for Interim and Final Management Orders on properties that would be eligible for licensing if necessary for the health, safety and welfare of the occupiers. These are similar to the orders that can be made on HMOs (for further details see page 154). Similar management orders can also be made on empty properties to bring them back into use.

Houses in multiple occupation (HMOs)

HMOs are defined as:

- A building where the flats are not self-contained, two or more (unrelated) occupiers share basic amenities such as a bathroom, toilet or cooking facilities, or the accommodation lacks one or more of those amenities. A self-contained flat can also be an HMO if unrelated occupiers share basic amenities, or the flat lacks one or more amenities.

- A building that has converted flats that are not all self-contained.
- A poorly converted block of flats that does not comply with the 1991 Building Regulations and where less than two-thirds of the flats are owner-occupied.
- Buildings such as some bed and breakfast hotels that partly provide accommodation for homeless people and partly for people on holiday. If the local authority is satisfied that a significant proportion of the building is used for the only or main home of some residents, then they can make a declaration that is it an HMO.

The new Housing Health and Safety Rating System (see page 135) also applies to HMOs. Local councils have extra powers they can use in HMOs. The powers cover:

- licensing
- management regulations
- management orders
- hazards
- overcrowding.

These are described in turn below.

Licensing of HMOs

There is a system of licensing private rented HMOs. Local authorities have to include in the licensing scheme all large HMOs, defined as buildings of three storeys or more with five occupants or more in two or more households. Local authorities also have a power, but not a duty, to apply licensing to other areas or categories of HMO.

To be licensed an HMO must fulfil a number of conditions:

- It must not house more than a maximum number of occupants, to prevent overcrowding.
- There must be satisfactory management arrangements for the HMO.

- The licence holder must be a fit and proper person, for example they should not have serious criminal convictions, or a history of bad management of rented housing.

- It must meet minimum standards on the quality of basic facilities including toilets, washing facilities and food preparation facilities.

- Landlords must abide by the conditions set down in the licence that must include supplying a copy of the annual Gas Safety Certificate, keeping electrical appliances and furnishings in a safe condition, and smoke alarms in working order. Authorities can also impose other conditions.

- Landlords must provide the occupiers with a written statement of the terms of their tenancy or other occupancy.

Licensing does not, however, apply to HMOs that have an interim or final management order on them (see page 154) or those that have been granted a temporary exemption by the local authority because the owner needs time to ensure the HMO will no longer need a licence.

Landlords who rent out an HMO that is covered by the scheme without a licence, face a number of penalties. They can be fined up to £20,000, can be required to repay up to a year's rent and housing benefit, and lose the right to an automatic possession order on assured shorthold tenancies.

Licences are valid for a maximum of five years. A licence can be revoked in certain circumstances.

Management regulations

All HMOs, not just those subject to licensing, must comply with national management regulations that cover fire precautions, water supply, and gas safety, repair and cleaning of common parts, furniture and waste storage.

Interim and Final Management Orders

Where a property ought to be licensed but there is no prospect of this happening in the near future, or a licence is being revoked, the local authority will have to apply to the Residential Property Tribunal to take over the management of the property with an Interim Management Order. They can also do this where the property is not licensable but there is a need to protect the health, safety or welfare of the occupiers. This can include a threat by the landlord to evict the occupiers in order to avoid licensing. The Interim Order can last for up to 12 months while the authority is putting in place long-term management arrangements. If the Interim Order is ending and the authority is unable to grant a licence, a Final Management Order must be made for a period of up to five years, to ensure proper long-term management of the property.

Other rights of tenants and long leaseholders 5

Introduction

In addition to protection from eviction and rights over repairs and rents, tenants have a wide variety of other rights. This chapter describes those rights.

Private tenants

Harassment and illegal eviction

Some landlords, if they cannot evict their tenants legally, will try to get them out by making life difficult, perhaps by withdrawing services such as gas and electricity, or by threatened or actual violence. This is known as harassment. If the landlord actually throws you out before s/he is entitled to, or changes the locks while you are out, this is known as illegal eviction. Most tenants and licensees are protected from both harassment and illegal eviction. You can also sue for damages and for an order allowing you to get back in.

There are two separate laws that protect tenants from harassment: the Protection from Eviction Act 1977 and the Protection from Harassment Act 1997. The 1977 Act is specifically designed to protect tenants and licensees, while the 1997 Act was originally passed to protect people from stalkers, but it can also be used in cases of racial harassment, neighbour disputes and harassment by landlords. It can be used in addition to, or instead of, the Protection from Eviction Act.

Protection from Eviction Act: who is protected

In addition to the protection for tenants under other laws set out in Chapter 2, the Protection from Eviction Act protects all residential occupiers. This covers the vast majority of people living in rented accommodation, including:

- all tenants and licensees continuing to live in the property after the tenancy or licence has ended.
- service occupiers with exclusive possession (see page 77), even after their contract of employment has ended.

While squatters are not covered by the Protection from Eviction Act, the landowner may commit an offence under other laws if any violence is used or threatened in the eviction, or if entry is forced into your home while you are inside.

Illegal eviction: who is protected

If your tenancy or licence began before 15 January 1989 and you are a residential occupier (see above), you are protected by the law against illegal eviction, meaning that your landlord will need to serve you with either a Notice to Quit, or a Notice Seeking Possession, depending on the type of tenancy you have. However, if your tenancy or licence began on or after 15 January 1989, or you have agreed a rent increase other than one set by a Rent Officer or Rent Tribunal, and you come into one of the following categories, then you will not be protected by the law against illegal eviction. Those who are excluded from protection are:

- people who share living accommodation with the landlord or landlord's family
- people who were originally squatters and who have been given a temporary tenancy or licence of the property
- people in a holiday letting
- licensees in a hostel provided by a local council, a housing association or some other public body
- people living in rent-free accommodation.

People in these circumstance are entitled only to reasonable notice from the landlord before eviction. All other tenants and licensees remain protected from illegal eviction, regardless of when their tenancy or licence began.

The Protection from Harassment Act

The Protection from Harassment Act covers a much wider range of harassment and it is not restricted only to residential occupiers. For these reasons it could be much more effective in preventing harassment. The penalties under the two Acts are similar.

What to do

If you suffer from harassment or illegal eviction, contact the tenancy relations officer, who is employed by the local council. The tenancy relations officer will normally try first to conciliate between you and your landlord, explaining the law to the landlord and that he or she is not allowed to harass you, or to evict you without going to court. If this is unsuccessful, the tenancy relations officer may then decide to prosecute the landlord. Unfortunately, however, courts often impose only very small fines on landlords and these do not deter the really unscrupulous ones. The court can also award compensation to you for personal injury, loss or damage.

In addition to action by the tenancy relations officer (or if your local council doesn't have a tenancy relations office), you can yourself take action through the civil courts. Seek advice before doing this. If you have a local law centre it is often best able to help on this sort of case. You or your adviser will be able to apply, usually to the county court, for an injunction. This is an order telling the landlord to stop harassing you and, if you have been illegally evicted, to let you back into your home. If the landlord disobeys this, s/he can be fined or sent to prison. If the case is urgent, you can go to the court for a temporary emergency order without the landlord being able to put his/her case forward. This is known as an *ex parte* injunction; it normally lasts only for a short period of up to a week, after which there will be another hearing with both parties present. At that hearing another order may be made, pending the full hearing of the case at which, if necessary, a final injunction will be granted. Along with the order, you can also ask for damages that could amount to several thousand pounds in certain circumstances.

Remember that good legal advice should always be sought. You might be entitled to free legal help (see pages 181–182). Your local law or housing aid centre is often best able to help in these sorts of cases.

When a tenant's family or partner can inherit the tenancy

If a tenancy is in joint names and one of the tenants dies, the other is automatically entitled to stay on as a tenant. When a fully protected regulated tenant (see page 67) dies and the tenancy was in that person's name only, the tenancy passes automatically to the spouse or civil partner, registered under the Civil Partnership Act 2004, of the deceased tenant. The surviving member of a couple who were living together but not married can also inherit the tenancy in this way. If there is no spouse or civil partner, then it passes to any member of the family who had been living in the home for at least two years prior to the tenant's death. However, that person will only have an assured tenancy (see page 58 for what this means). When an assured tenant dies, the tenancy passes to their spouse or civil partner or to the surviving member of a couple who were living together. This right to inherit the tenancy is known as succeeding to the tenancy and in the case of an assured tenancy there is the right to only one such succession. So the original tenant can be followed by one further tenant who succeeds to the tenancy. In the case of a regulated tenancy (see above) there can be two such successions.

The right to a rent book and receipts for rent

If you have a weekly tenancy and you are not provided with substantial board (see page 68), you have a legal right to a rent book from the landlord. No other tenants or licensees have this right. The tenancy relations officer of the local council can prosecute if the landlord refuses to provide a rent book to a tenant who is entitled to one. The rent book must contain information on the name and address of the landlord and agent (if any), on the rent payable, on your rights to have a rent fixed, on your protection from eviction, and to your right to claim housing benefit.

If you are not entitled to a rent book from your landlord, try to get receipts or at least pay by cheque, so that the payment is recorded. This is important in case the landlord later tries to claim that you have not paid the rent. If the landlord will only take cash and refuses to give receipts, try to pay in the presence of a witness. Write to the landlord to request a receipt and keep a copy of the letter.

When the landlord can enter your home

Landlords have the right to enter occasionally to inspect the property for any repairs that they are obliged to carry out. However s/he should give you at least 24 hours' notice and arrange to visit at a reasonable time of day. If the landlord is persistently entering without your permission, s/he may be trespassing and you may be able to take legal action to prevent it.

If you do not want your landlord to make improvements

If your landlord is planning to make improvements to your home and you do not want them done, you may be able to prevent them if you are a fully protected tenant (see page 67). The landlord can only make improvements against your wishes if:

- your tenancy agreement states that s/he can do so
- the landlord has applied for an improvement grant from the local council, it is likely to be approved and s/he has been to court to get permission to carry out the improvements against your wishes. You can dispute the landlord's plans in court and in reaching a decision the judge will take into account your age and health, what accommodation

arrangements will be made for you while the work is carried out and the inconvenience to you

- the landlord is legally obliged to carry out the work.

If you have to move out during the building work, make sure that your right to return to the property is agreed in writing by the landlord. Seek advice before agreeing to any proposals by the landlord or before deciding to dispute them.

A list of furniture

If the tenancy is furnished you should arrange to agree with the landlord a list of the furniture provided. This is known as an inventory. It should include a note on the condition of each item. This should help to prevent future disputes about any damage to the furniture. Normally, the landlord does not have to provide an inventory by law, unless you paid a lump sum for the furniture at the beginning of the tenancy. If the landlord refuses to supply one, you could make your own and send a copy, asking him/her to tell you if there are any inaccuracies.

No children allowed

Many landlords say that no children are allowed. If this is part of your tenancy agreement and you have children, or bring them to live with you, then you will be breaking your agreement. However, if the landlord goes to court to evict you and you are a fully protected or assured tenant, you could claim that it is not reasonable to evict you for this reason (see page 67 for protected tenants and page 58 for assured tenants). If the landlord made no mention of children not being allowed at the beginning of the tenancy, s/he cannot later use it as a ground for trying to evict you.

If, however, you bring children into the accommodation and thereby cause illegal overcrowding, you might be evicted on these grounds (see page 149 for more details of overcrowding and the circumstances in which it is permitted).

Changing the tenancy agreement

There is nothing to stop the landlord and tenant agreeing to change the terms of the tenancy at any time. But the key word here is agreement. Both sides must agree any change and one side cannot impose a change on the other. If the landlord does ask you to sign a new agreement at any time after you have moved in, get advice before signing anything because you could be reducing your legal rights by entering into a new agreement. You do not have to sign anything and, if you do not, the terms of the old agreement will continue to apply.

If you are a regulated tenant and you sign an agreement to pay a higher rent, this does not prevent you from later applying to the Rent Officer for a fair rent to be fixed (see page 106). The agreement to increase the rent must be in writing and must state at the top that you do not have to sign the agreement, that your security will not be affected if you do not and that you can apply to the Rent Officer for a fair rent to be fixed at any time.

Fuel costs: what landlords can charge

If you pay your landlord for the use of gas and electricity, there is a maximum amount that s/he can charge for each unit of fuel you use set down by the industry regulator OFGEM (see Useful contacts on page 197). If you think you have been overcharged, seek advice, because you can recover any excess.

Unfair contracts and tenancy agreements

A condition in a contract or agreement between you and a landlord or accommodation agency might be invalid if it is unfair to you. Examples of unfair terms in a tenancy agreement might include excessive penalty charges for late payment of rent, charges that make you pay the landlord's costs, or giving the landlord a right to enter your home without giving reasonable notice. Written contracts must be in plain and intelligible language which is understandable without having to go to a lawyer. The Unfair Terms Unit of the Office of Fair Trading will investigate any possible unfair terms referred to it (see Useful contacts on page 197).

Private tenants and long leaseholders

Private tenants and people who own their home on a long lease (usually flatowners) have a range of rights covering the ownership and management of their homes and the common parts. Leaseholders can get further information on all of these from the Leasehold Advisory Service (see Useful contacts on page 196).

Buying the freehold of the building from the landlord

Private tenants and long leaseholders have a right of first refusal if their landlord wants to sell the freehold of their building. This right does not apply, however, to assured tenants (see page 58), tenants of resident landlords (see page 68) or service tenants (see page 78). To qualify as resident for this purpose the landlord must have lived in a flat in the building as his/her only or main home for at least a year before selling the freehold. However, the landlord does not count as resident if the building was originally built as a block of flats.

If the landlord sells the property without first offering it to the tenants, they can be prosecuted and long leaseholders can require the new owner to sell it to them for the same price.

You have the right to buy the freehold of your house or flat from the landlord, usually for a very low sum, or to extend the lease beyond the date it ended. You must have been living there as your only or main home for at least one year or for three out of the last ten years.

In the case of flats, the right to buy the freehold only applies to groups of leaseholders in self-contained buildings of two or more flats, where at least two-thirds of the flats are owned on long leases and at least half are participating in the purchase. Some properties are excluded:

- those containing non-residential premises (for example, a shop) that exceed 25 per cent of the total floor area
- buildings with a resident landlord that contain no more than four flats

- buildings where the landlord can show the intent to demolish a substantial part of it in the next five years.

The price of buying the freehold can be fixed by agreement or, if you cannot agree with the landlord, by the Leasehold Valuation Tribunal. If you are thinking of buying you should seek legal advice. You should get together with the other occupants of the building and seek legal advice if you want to buy from the landlord under one of these procedures.

Commonhold

People who own their home on a long lease can now transfer to a new form of ownership known as commonhold. This means that they own their own homes individually, and jointly own the remainder; for example the common parts in a block of flats, through a company known as a commonhold association. Some of the advantages are that there is no landlord, the residents are in control and it avoids the problem of the value of leases reducing as the term runs down. It is also legally simpler, without the need for complicated individual leases for each property.

The right to a management audit

Long leaseholders who pay variable service charges have the right to arrange an audit by a qualified surveyor or accountant of all the management functions carried out by their landlord. They have to pay the cost of the audit. It examines whether the landlord is managing the property efficiently and effectively, including whether the service charges are value for money.

The right to manage the property

Leaseholders have a right to take over management of their block if it contains two or more flats and at least two-thirds of the flats are held on long leases.

If the landlord has failed to manage the property properly, including failure to carry out repairs, then tenants and long leaseholders can apply to the Leasehold Valuation Tribunal to appoint a manager to carry out these duties. This right does not apply to assured tenants (see page 58) or tenants of resident landlords.

Changing the lease

Owners of leasehold properties whose lease is longer than 21 years can apply to change the lease if it does not contain satisfactory arrangements for repairs, insurance, or service charges. Seek legal advice if you believe your lease is inadequate.

The right to know the name of the landlord

You have a legal right to know the name of your landlord. If you cannot find out the landlord's name, write to the person who last collected rent from you stating that you are requesting a written statement of the landlord's full name and address and pointing out that you have a right to this information under Part VI of the Landlord and Tenant Act 1987. Send the letter by recorded delivery so they cannot deny having received it, and keep copies of all correspondence. If the landlord's agent fails to respond to this, the tenancy relations officer (see page 157) can prosecute them and you may be able to withhold rent or service charges under certain circumstances, but get advice before doing so. You can also get details of your landlord from your local Land Registry; look for the address in the telephone directory.

Council and housing association tenants

Most council tenants are secure tenants and have a range of additional rights under the Housing Act 1985. Housing association tenants whose tenancy began before 15 January 1989 are usually also secure tenants and have the same legal rights as council tenants. Those whose tenancy began on or after that date are usually assured tenants (see page 58). They do not have the same rights set down in law, but most of the rights described in this section should be spelt out for them in their tenancy agreement.

The right to inherit the tenancy

If the tenancy is in joint names and one of the tenants dies, the other automatically stays on as tenant. If the tenancy is in one person's name and that person dies, it passes to their spouse or civil partner (if they have been living together) or to another member of the family who has been living with the tenant for at least a year before the tenant died. This is known as the right to succeed to the tenancy and applies to all of the following: husband, wife, civil partner, parent, grandparent, child, grandchild, brother, sister, uncle, aunt, nephew, niece, stepchild, illegitimate child, and couples living together as man and wife but are not married. Relationships by marriage and half-relationships also count.

These rights to succeed to the tenancy only apply to one succession, and if the tenancy is passed from joint tenants to one of the tenants, this too counts as a succession. After one succession, it is up to the landlord whether you can stay or not. So, for example, if a man had the tenancy in his name and died, his wife would have the right to succeed, but when she died any remaining family members would not have that right, although the landlord may agree to let them stay on. If you are the spouse or civil partner of the deceased tenant and you succeed to the tenancy, the landlord cannot then try to move you to smaller accommodation. If, however, you are another member of the family, or you were not married to your partner, and you succeed to the tenancy, the landlord can ask the court for permission to move you to suitable alternative accommodation, but only if they can prove that your present home is larger than you reasonably need and if they give you written notice of their intention to do this between six and 12 months after the original tenant's death (see page 95 for more details).

The right to take in lodgers and tenants

If you want to rent out part of your home, different rules apply depending on whether you let it to a lodger or to a tenant. The legal difference is that a lodger is only a licensee. The difference depends on the degree of control you keep over rooms that are let out. If you share living accommodation and eat together the person is almost certainly a lodger. If you let a self-contained part of your home, do not share any rooms with the person you let to and do not provide them with any food or services such as cleaning, that person will probably be a tenant (see page 56 for more details on the differences between licensees and tenants).

You have the right to take in lodgers without getting your landlord's permission. You also have the right to let a part of your home (but not all of it) to a tenant, but must first get your landlord's written permission. The landlord cannot refuse permission without giving good reasons in writing. If they do refuse permission you can challenge this in the county court. It is up to the landlord to prove they are being reasonable. They might, for example, argue that it would lead to overcrowding of the property. If you do decide to take in a lodger or tenant, both they and you will have certain legal rights and obligations and you should make sure you understand these before going ahead. See Chapter 2 for further details.

Passing on the tenancy to someone else

You are not normally allowed to pass the tenancy on to someone else. The only exceptions to this are:

- when you exercise your right to exchange tenancies (see page 25)
- when property is transferred by the court to one partner after a divorce or other proceedings under the Children Act
- when the person to whom you pass the tenancy is a member of your family who would have the right to succeed to the tenancy after your death. However, if you do pass on the tenancy in this way, no one else will then have a right to succeed to the tenancy after that person's death (see page 165 on the right to inherit the tenancy). The law in this area is complicated and you should get legal advice if you are thinking of passing on your tenancy in this way.

You can only pass on the tenancy (which is known as assigning the tenancy) in one of these three circumstances. See page 25 for details on the right to exchange with another tenant.

The right to be consulted by the landlord

Secure tenants (but not tenants of county councils) have a right to be consulted by their landlord on all matters of housing management that might affect them substantially. This would cover, for example, repair programmes or caretaking arrangements, but does not include rent increases. Landlords are free to decide how to carry out these consultations and must publish details of how they will consult tenants. The details must be available for tenants to examine free of charge, and copies must be on sale at a reasonable cost. If new policies or practices are introduced without tenants being consulted, then the landlord is breaking the law. However, once they have consulted tenants, landlords are free to go ahead with their plans even if the tenants disagree.

Changes to the tenancy agreement

All the rights described in this section are written into the Housing Act 1985. Landlords cannot reduce or remove them by anything that is put in your tenancy agreement. If they want to change your tenancy agreement, they have to give you a written notice in advance, stating what changes they want to make and giving you a reasonable period in which to comment on them. However, once they have consulted you, even if you disagree with the change, they can still go ahead with it. Once they decide to go ahead, they must serve a notice of variation giving at least four weeks' notice of the change.

Rights to information

Landlords must provide you with a simple written explanation of your rights under the Housing Act 1985 described in this section, and of their duties to carry out repairs. They must also provide you with a written explanation of your rights and obligations under the tenancy agreement.

Landlords must publish a summary of the rules they apply in deciding who should be offered housing and which tenants should be offered transfers. The full set of rules should be available at a reasonable charge. Landlords must provide anyone who asks with a free copy of a summary of the rules. You also have the right to check that any information you have given to the landlord about an application for housing or transfer has been accurately recorded.

The Right to Buy

Most council and housing association tenants have the right to buy their home. Full details are available from your landlord. Before deciding to take up the Right to Buy, make sure that you know all the extra costs involved and that you can afford them now and in the future. In addition to mortgage payments you will have to pay water rates, insurance, service charges if in a flat, and all repair and maintenance costs. If you suffer a drop in income in future you may find there is no extra help available to meet your housing costs.

Unfair tenancy agreements

Council and housing association tenants have the same rights to dispute unfair terms in their tenancy agreements as private tenants (see page 161).

Making a complaint

If you are unhappy with the service provided by your landlord, you should first contact the office that you usually deal with and ask them to sort it out.

If they fail to do so, or you are not happy with their explanation, you should tell the office you want to make a complaint and ask for details of their complaints procedure. This will usually involve taking the problem to a manager who will review and try to resolve it.

If you are still unhappy, your next step will depend on what type of landlord you have.

- If you are a council tenant, you can complain to your local councillor. You can find out their name from the Town Hall. If the councillor cannot resolve the problem, you can complain to the Local Government Ombudsman (in Wales, the Public Services Ombudsman for Wales – see page 144).

- If you are a tenant of a housing association or other registered social landlord, you can complain to the Independent Housing Ombudsman (in Wales, the Public Services Ombudsman for Wales) who will investigate and try to resolve your complaint (see Useful contacts on pages 195 and 198).

Housing rights and relationship breakdown 6

Introduction

When the relationship of a couple who have been married or living together breaks down, there are sometimes problems over which of them has the right to live in the home. The rights of partners depend on whether or not they are married or have registered a civil partnership under the Civil Partnership Act 2004, on the custody arrangements for any children, and their legal status in the home. When a relationship breaks down there are many difficult personal decisions to be made. This chapter deals only with the housing aspects of the problems. For further advice on other problems, see Chapter 7 and *Relationship breakdown: housing rights for couples who are splitting up* (published by Shelter). The rights described in this chapter apply equally to married couples and to civil partners. Where action in connection with divorce is referred to this is shorthand not only for divorce proceedings but also for judicial separation and nullity proceedings.

In an emergency

If you live with someone who threatens you, or is violent to you or your children, you may need to take action quickly. Going to a refuge is one possibility – see page 47 for details. The sections below detail the other possibilities open to you.

Going to the council

You can go to the council and ask for help as a homeless person. Local councils have duties to help homeless people; for further details see page 12. However, some local councils demand proof of violence and you may need to get evidence from a professional person, such as a doctor or social worker, or from the police if they have been involved.

Some councils might say that you are not homeless, or that they do not have a duty to you, because you could get a court order to protect you, even though these are often useless in preventing violence. Seek advice if the local council is refusing to help you.

Even if you are not counted as being in priority need (see page 13), some councils will offer accommodation to all battered women/ men, but there is no legal obligation for them to do so.

A battered woman/man who has had to leave home because of violence or threats of violence should never be regarded as having become intentionally homeless. Seek advice if the council says that you are intentionally homeless.

If you are accepted as homeless by a local council away from your home area, you should not be sent back to your original council area for housing if there is a risk of violence in that area.

Getting a court order

The other course of action you can take in an emergency is to get a court order against the person you live with. These orders can do a number of things. They can order the person:

- not to assault or harass you
- not to assault any children living with you
- to leave the home and not to return
- to keep a certain distance from your home or any other place you or your children go regularly
- to let you back into your home if s/he has excluded you.

If you believe a court order like this would help you, you should seek advice immediately on where to find a solicitor or law centre. Your solicitor will be able to apply for an order. The law applies equally whether or not you are married to the person you live with.

The courts regard exclusion orders, which forbid the person to enter the home, as very serious measures. If the person owns the home where you are living, or if the tenancy is in his/her name only, it is difficult to get anything more than a short-term exclusion order. In such cases, the court is likely to put a time limit on the order, probably of no more than three months. However, if you have the tenancy or ownership of the property in your name only, you should be able to get a permanent exclusion order, and you may also be able to get a permanent order if you are joint tenants.

If the person disobeys the order, s/he is disobeying the court and is in contempt of court. This means that s/he can be brought back to court again and the judge can alter the terms of the order to try to make it more effective, or can order the person to be imprisoned. It is likely, however, that the court will be willing on the first occasion to accept a promise of good conduct in the future. If the person is imprisoned, s/he may be released after a short time if s/he apologises to the court for his/her behaviour.

An order is likely to be more effective if a power of arrest is attached. This can be done if the judge is satisfied that there has been actual bodily harm and that this is likely to happen again. The power of arrest enables the police to arrest the person without a warrant if they have reasonable cause to believe that s/he has disobeyed the order. If a power of arrest is attached to the order, make sure that a copy of the order has been sent to the local police station so that they know in advance that they might have to take action. However, the police are not obliged to arrest the person even if there is further trouble, and they can often be reluctant to become involved in domestic disputes.

If the problem is urgent, or you do not want the person to know that you are taking legal action because s/he is likely to become more violent, you can go straight to court without him/her being informed. Because the person does not have an opportunity to put forward his/her case, the order will only be a temporary one until a full hearing can be arranged, in perhaps a week's time, when both sides can put forward their cases. It is more difficult to get an exclusion order without the other person knowing in advance unless there is very clear evidence of violence. Courts are also reluctant to attach a power of arrest in such cases.

Problems with court orders

It may be that an order will help to protect you, but there are problems with them. They are usually only temporary; they cannot normally, for example, deprive the person permanently of any legal rights s/he might have to the home. Some men/women are not deterred by an order and may indeed be incited to further violence. Sometimes local councils pressurise people into applying for an order as an alternative to being housed by the council. No one has the right to insist that you apply for an order and, if this happens to you, you should get advice.

Long-term rights to the home

Your long-term rights to stay in the home depend on whether or not you are married to your partner or have a registered civil partnership and on the present legal rights of each of you to the home.

If you are married or have a civil partnership

If you are married or have a registered civil partnership, and your tenancy or ownership of the home is in joint names, you have equal rights to live in the home and, if it is owner-occupied, to a share of the proceeds if it is sold. For this reason, couples are usually best advised to have their tenancy or ownership in joint names. You may in certain circumstances (see below) have a right to more (or less) than a half share, or to the tenancy in your name after the divorce.

If you are married or a civil partner but the ownership or tenancy is in one name only, there are laws to protect the rights of the other partner.

The court has the power to decide who has ownership or rights over the matrimonial or partnership home, even if the property is held in the name of only one person. This can also apply to people who have been married but are now divorced and to people who were planning to get married within three years of their engagement.

Spouses or civil partners who are not the owner or tenant of the home have the right to live there. The court has the power to exclude either of the spouses or partners, even if they are the sole or joint owner or tenant. If your spouse or partner has left and stopped paying the rent or mortgage repayments, the landlord or lender is obliged to accept the payments from you (if you wish to make them) even though the home is not in your name. If your home is owned by your spouse or partner you can register your right to live in it. This prevents your spouse or partner selling the home before the court has decided who has a right to it and also prevents him/her from taking out a second mortgage on the property without your knowledge. This is known as registering a charge on the home. You should ask your solicitor to do it immediately. The court also has power to transfer a fully protected private tenancy (see page 67), an assured tenancy (see page 58), or a council or housing association secure tenancy (see page 90) from one partner to the other.

If the matrimonial or partnership home is owner-occupied and proceedings have started for a divorce, the court will decide how the value of the property should be divided up. The law recognises that, even if the home is in one partner's name only, the other has a right to a share in its value; for example, a married woman may have made a large unpaid contribution through housework and child care and this should be recognised in divorce proceedings. The court looks at a number of things to decide how much you should get. The first consideration must be given to any children of the marriage while they are under 18. After that, the court looks at:

- The income and resources of both you and your partner. This can include any income you are likely to have, or could reasonably be expected to get, in the future. This means that the court may look at your future earning capacity and may consider that it is reasonable to expect you to go back to work in the future. It may be that you will have to provide evidence of the lack of employment opportunities in the area.

- The needs of you and your partner. This means what you need to live on, and what your partner's needs are (for example, if they have remarried and have a second family to support).

- The standard of living that you and your partner had before your relationship broke down.

- Your ages, and how long the relationship lasted.

- Any physical or mental disabilities affecting you or your partner.

- Any contributions that you and your partner have made to the welfare of the family and any contributions that you are likely to make in the future. This means, if you have custody of the children, the court will take into account the fact that you will be looking after them.

- The conduct of you and your partner. The behaviour of you and your partner will only be taken into account if the court thinks that it would be unfair to ignore it.

- The loss of any benefits that you might have had if the relationship had not broken down (for example, any pension scheme that your partner may belong to).

The court also has to consider whether there is any way that they can make a 'clean break' between you and your partner. This means ensuring that there would be no further financial ties between you and your partner.

In certain circumstances, the court can order the sale of the home and the distribution of the money raised between the partners.

The court can also order that one partner has the right to live in the property indefinitely or for a particular period (for example, until a change of circumstances such as remarriage), after which it will be sold and the proceeds divided as the court decides. This is commonly used to ensure that a woman who has custody of the children has a home to bring them up in. If you are not married or in a civil partnership, your rights depend on who is the tenant or owner of the home.

Tenants

If you have a joint tenancy in both your names then you both have equal rights to the home. You can exclude your partner temporarily if s/he is violent or threatening violence by getting an order (see page 172). It is possible, although not usual, to get a court order to exclude him/her indefinitely from a joint tenancy. You will probably have to try to reach agreement on who should stay. If you are a council tenant you may be able to get the council to rehouse one of you. Get advice on rehousing by the council from an independent agency (see page 181). Do not just give up a tenancy, because you may find the council will later decide that you are intentionally homeless and refuse to help you.

If the tenancy is in your or your partner's name only, then the other person can apply for the right to stay there, and for their partner to be excluded and the tenancy to be transferred. If there has been violence or the threat of violence, you can get the person excluded temporarily while you find another place to live (see In an emergency on page 171). Get advice immediately because, if your partner wants you to leave, you can also apply to the local council as a homeless person. See page 12 to find out whether you might be entitled to rehousing by the council. If there is no violence, or your partner will not evict you, you will probably find it difficult to persuade the council to help you, and you should get advice.

Homeowners

If you live in an owner-occupied home, you and your partner may have certain rights to a share of the property even if you are not married. These rights have been established over many years in the courts, but there are no specific Acts of Parliament to protect you.

If the home is jointly owned, you have a clear right to a share in its value. If you have contributed equally towards buying and maintaining it, you would normally be entitled to a half-share. If, however, one of you has contributed more than the other, that person may be entitled to more than half. The court cannot order the property to be transferred to one partner or the other, but it does have the power to order it to be sold so that each partner gets their share. However, if you want to stay in the property you could try to raise another mortgage to buy out your partner's share.

If your home is in your partner's name, you have no automatic right to live there, even if the relationship has lasted a long time and there are children. However, you can get a solicitor to argue in court that the purpose of your partner in setting up the home was to provide for you and any children. You might also be able to show that you have contributed to the property, either by helping with mortgage repayments or perhaps putting up money for a deposit, or by helping with maintenance or improvement of the property (day-to-day housework does not count). If any of these circumstances apply, you might be able to go to court to argue that your partner holds the property on trust for you. This will give you a right to a share in the value of the property that will be decided by the court. If you are going to court to argue this, you should make sure that your solicitor registers your claim on the property (see page 175), so your partner cannot sell it before the case comes to court.

If the house is only in your name, the same points will apply as if the house was only in your partner's name (see above).

Money problems

If your relationship is breaking down there are a number of money problems you might have to sort out.

- **Maintenance for yourself**: if you are married, you can make an application for maintenance payments for yourself, and for changes in the amount paid at any time during the marriage, or after it is finished. The court considers the resources available to each partner. Decisions over maintenance are tied up with decisions over the future of your home, because transfer of a tenancy or ownership of the home to you may form part of the arrangements for future maintenance. You might settle for a transfer of the home in return for lower money payments. Consult your solicitor, who will be concerned to get the best arrangement for you. If you are not married you cannot claim any maintenance payments for yourself.

- **Maintenance for your children**: whether or not you are married to the other parent, you can claim child support maintenance from him/her under the Child Support Act 1991 (and you may also have to claim child support maintenance if you are on benefits). The Child Support Agency will calculate the amount of maintenance payable.

- **Rent arrears**: if you or your partner have got into rent arrears, the responsibility for paying off the arrears will depend on who is the tenant. If the tenancy is in one name only, that person is responsible for the arrears and the other partner cannot be made to pay them. So if, for example, the tenancy was in your partner's name only and s/he has run up arrears, you are not responsible for paying them. If the tenancy is in joint names, you are both equally liable. If, however, you are the tenant of a public landlord such as a local authority or housing association, but in practice your partner took responsibility for paying the rent and ran up arrears without your knowledge, you could try asking your landlord to write off the arrears. They do not have to do this, but they may treat your problems sympathetically.

- **Mortgage arrears**: if you or your partner have mortgage arrears, read the advice on page 120.

- **Loss of income**: if you have suffered a loss of income because of relationship breakdown, you may well qualify for extra welfare benefits. Seek advice and see Useful publications on page 191.

Your children

Decisions will have to be made about where any children you have will live (known as the residence of children) and arrangements for contact with them. People often worry that if they do not have an adequate home, or if the home is in their partner's name, they might not be able to keep the children with them. This should not affect your chances because:

- The court awards residence according to its judgment of the best interests of the children. The most important factor is who is closest to them and best able to look after them. Housing is only one point to be taken into account.

- The court will often decide to award the right to stay in the matrimonial home to whoever is the best person to look after the children.

- If you are in danger of becoming homeless and have the children with you, the local council may well have a responsibility to find a home for you (see page 12).

Key points to remember

- If your relationship is breaking down and your home is at risk, seek legal advice from a solicitor or legal centre immediately. You may be able to get help with legal costs (see page 184).

- You may have a right to keep up rent and mortgage payments, even if the home is in your partner's name and s/he has left you.

- You may have a right to stay in the home either temporarily or permanently, and have it transferred to your name, even if at present it is in your partner's name.

Getting advice and legal representation

7

Introduction

This chapter tells you where to go for further advice and help. Addresses and telephone numbers of the organisations listed can be found in Useful contacts on pages 193–199. You can get details of your local advice centres by calling Shelter's free housing advice helpline on 0808 800 4444 (open seven days a week from 8am to midnight; charges may apply if you ring from a mobile phone) or visit www.shelter.org.uk/adviceonline

General advice

The nationwide network of Citizens Advice Bureaux provides advice on all problems including housing, legal matters, welfare benefits and relationship breakdown. If necessary, they can refer you for more detailed help to specialist agencies or to a solicitor. The advice service is free of charge. In some areas there are neighbourhood centres that offer free advice services, often based in shops in high streets or shopping centres. To find your local office look in the telephone directory under Citizens Advice Bureau or visit www.adviceguide.org.uk

Housing advice centres

In many areas there are specialist centres offering housing aid and advice. The service they offer varies from one-off information, to detailed help over a long period. There are two main types:

- Local council housing aid centres: these can advise on all problems. However, they will not usually be able to take action against their own local council. If you have a problem with the local council, its housing aid centre may be able to discuss the matter with other sections of the council but will not, for example, be able to take legal action against it. So if you have a dispute with the council (for example, over repairs, or because it will not accept you as a homeless person), it would be more beneficial for you to go to an independent advice centre.

- Independent housing aid centres: these can often offer detailed assistance over a period of time. These centres usually cover all types of housing problems and offer their services free of charge. There are a number of housing aid centres throughout the country operated by Shelter (to find your nearest centre visit www.shelter.org.uk/adviceonline or ring Shelter's free housing advice helpline on 0808 800 4444 – charges may apply if you ring from a mobile phone).

Other specialist advice

- **Law Centres**: these give free legal advice and can sometimes represent you in court. They usually advise on all aspects of housing law and can help with orders for battered women. They cannot, however, take on divorce cases, for which you will need a solicitor. Shelter can give you details of local law centres (see above).

- **Welfare rights**: for advice on welfare rights, try your local council, which may employ a welfare rights officer. Advisers can also contact the Advice Line run by the Child Poverty Action Group on 020 7833 4627 or visit www.cpag.org.uk

- **Debt**: National Debtline provides free, confidential and independent advice over the telephone on 0808 808 4000 (charges may apply if you ring from a mobile phone) and online at www.nationaldebtline.co.uk

- **Lone parents**: One Parent Families/Gingerbread is a national organisation for single parents that offers advice on all problems, including housing, social security and divorce through its free Lone Parent Helpline 0800 018 5026 (charges may apply if you ring from a mobile phone), or by visiting www.oneparentfamilies.org.uk

- **Women's rights**: the Women's Aid Federation England (0808 200 0247; www.womensaid.org.uk) and Welsh Women's Aid (0808 80 10 800; www.welshwomensaid.org) refer women (with or without children) to refuges. They give advice on court orders, divorce, housing and social security. They can put you in touch with sympathetic solicitors and local women's aid groups.

- **Race and sex discrimination**: the Equality and Human Rights Commission (020 7215 8415; www.equalityhumanrights.com) can give advice and help on action against sex and racial discrimination.

- **Immigration**: the United Kingdom Immigrants Advisory Service (www.iasuk.org) offers advice and help with immigration problems. The Joint Council for the Welfare of Immigrants (020 7251 8708; www.jcwi.org.uk) offers advice and help on all types of problems concerned with immigration and nationality. The Refugee Council (020 7346 6700; www.refugeecouncil.org.uk) has an advice service for refugees and asylum seekers.

Many areas have local Community Relations Councils (CRCs) that can also help and advise. You can get the address of your local CRC from local advice centres.

Solicitors

Solicitors can advise you on all aspects of the law, represent you in certain courts and, if necessary, find a barrister to represent you. However, it is best to find a solicitor who specialises in the area of the law that is relevant to your problem (not all, for example, are experts on the law protecting private tenants, or equally expert at getting a court order for battered women). You may be able to claim free legal help. You can find a list of solicitors who specialise in housing law from the Law Society website (www.lawsociety.org.uk/choosingandusing/ findasolicitor.law), the Community Legal Service (CLS) Directory in your local library, or the CLS website (www.clsdirect.org.uk). If you do not know a good solicitor, contact one of the advice agencies listed above and ask for a recommendation.

Free advice and help

The Legal Help scheme can pay for the cost of your solicitor writing letters, negotiating on your behalf and obtaining advice from a barrister about your case. Under it, you can get up to two hours' worth of advice and assistance from a solicitor. For matrimonial cases, the limit is three hours' work and in all cases, the solicitor can extend the amount of time spent working on your case, in some circumstances by up to five hours.

Your solicitor will be able to advise you on whether your level of income allows you to qualify for help under this scheme.

In addition, many solicitors also operate a free or low-cost interview scheme, under which anyone, regardless of their income, can get limited advice.

Publicly funded legal representation

This covers all types of legal costs, including the cost of going to court. Your solicitor will help you fill in an application form. It will normally take some weeks for the application to be processed and it will not be possible to start court proceedings until the certificate is granted. However, in urgent cases, for example, obtaining a court order to exclude a violent partner from your home, an application for emergency public funding (formerly known as legal aid) can be made. Where urgent representation is needed, a solicitor may be able to get emergency legal funds.

To qualify for help, you have to pass two tests:

- You must come within the financial limits of the scheme, which takes both income and savings into account. Your local advice centre should be able to give you an idea of whether you qualify and roughly what contribution, if any, you would have to make. If you are married or in a civil partnership and living with your spouse/partner, and not in dispute with him/her, your income and capital will be added together to work out whether you qualify for help.

- You also have to have reasonable grounds for taking, or defending, the action. This will be decided by the Legal Services Commission, which administers the scheme. It will not prejudge the rights and wrongs of your case, but simply decide whether it is reasonable to spend public funds on pursuing it.

The statutory charge

There is one particular feature of the scheme that it is vital for anybody who seeks help to understand. If you succeed in recovering or retaining money or property (including, for example, a house where there has been a dispute over who has the right to it) then you may, in addition to your initial contribution to any costs, have to pay an extra sum for legal costs. This extra sum is known as the Statutory Charge, and your solicitor should fully explain this to you.

Special rules apply in matrimonial cases – maintenance and the first £3,000 of any money or property settlement is exempt from the charge.

When it is property, rather than cash, that has been recovered or retained, the Legal Services Commission has the discretion not to insist on immediate payment of any money due to it, and to transfer the charge to a different property. It is the practice to wait until the house is sold before recovering the money or even, in some cases, to agree to transfer the charge to another house, which means it stays as an outstanding debt. This may be agreed if there is at least one dependent child who will be living with you in the second house, or if the reason for the move is to do with health, disability or employment, and a refusal would cause hardship. Obviously, the equity in the second house must be sufficient to cover the amount owed to the Commission.

There have been a number of occasions in recent years where people have been involved in a prolonged and expensive dispute over property and in the end have been left with very little of the sum awarded to them because of the way in which the charge operates. Because of the large extra costs for which you might become liable, it is always worth making every effort to negotiate a settlement prior to a court hearing, rather than fighting the matter out in court.

Campaigning to change policies

Housing problems are not only tackled by individual action, indeed, in some circumstances you may be able to solve your own problem more quickly and effectively by collective rather than individual action. One example is the problem of getting local councils to carry out repairs, where tenants' associations can often be far more effective than any individual. You may wish to share your experiences with other people who have had similar problems, or help to campaign for better housing policies from local councils, or the Government. The section below gives you information on campaigning organisations you can contact. Their addresses and telephone numbers are listed under Useful contacts on pages 193–199.

General campaigns

Shelter (www.shelter.org.uk), the housing and homelessness charity, has a network of housing aid centres and special projects that help homeless and badly housed people. It also campaigns and undertakes research on all issues connected with housing.

Homeless Link (www.homeless.org.uk) is the membership body for organisations and individuals providing services and support to homeless people.

Council tenants

Contact your local tenants' association.

Private tenants

Contact a local tenants' or residents' association if there is one.

Homelessness

The Homelessness Act 2002 gave local housing authorities a new duty to produce local homelessness strategies. They must consult with local voluntary organisations and interested individuals and publish the strategy. This offers the opportunity to influence local programmes to tackle homelessness. Contact Homeless Link for details of local groups in your area (see Useful contacts on page 195).

Welfare rights

Child Poverty Action Group (www.cpag.org.uk) researches and campaigns on poverty and welfare rights. Individuals and groups can join as members.

Appendices

Appendix 1: Useful publications

Publications listed here can be obtained through bookshops or, particularly in the case of those produced by voluntary organisations, directly from the publishers.

General housing law

Shelter housing law update is a monthly bulletin of the latest developments in housing law and policy. For information on how to subscribe, or for a free trial copy, visit www.shelter.org.uk/shlu

For advisers who need greater detail on housing law the following are highly recommended:

Shelter Legal is a comprehensive and up-to-date housing law information resource available online. It covers all aspects of housing, explaining how the legislation and case law work in practice in a way that is accessible and relevant to those working in every area of housing law. For information on how to subscribe, or for a free trial, visit www.shelter.org.uk/legal

Manual of Housing Law, Andrew Arden and Caroline Hunter (Sweet and Maxwell)
For housing advisers, lawyers and others with some familiarity with housing law, this is a practical handbook for everyday reference.

Encyclopaedia of Housing Law and Practice, general editor Andrew Arden (Sweet and Maxwell)
Five volumes of legislation, rules, orders and circulars. As legislation and regulations are amended frequently, anyone wishing to check on the current state of the law will find this encyclopaedia indispensable. It includes explanatory commentary, and is also available on CD-ROM.

Chapter 1

Flat Owners' Guide Paul Walentowicz with Charlie Robinson (Shelter) see www.shelter.org.uk/publications

Homelessness Code of Guidance for Local Authorities (CLG) available to download at: www.communities.gov.uk/publications/housing/homelessnesscode

Buy, Sell and Move House (Which?) see www.which.co.uk

Shared Ownership (Housing Corporation)
Free leaflet on housing association shared ownership schemes. Available to download at: www.housingcorp.gov.uk

London Homelessness Directory – Hostels and Supported Accommodation (formerly the London Hostels Directory) (Resource Information Service) see www.ris.org.uk

Squatters' Handbook (Advisory Service for squatters) see www.squatter.org.uk

Shelter Guide: Finding a place to live (Shelter) see www.shelter.org.uk/publications

Shelter Guide: Private tenancies: paying a deposit (Shelter) see www.shelter.org.uk/publications

Asylum seekers: a guide to recent legislation (Resource Information Service) see www.ris.org.uk

Chapter 2

Defending Possession Proceedings 6th edition, Nic Madge, Derek McConnell, John Gallagher and Jan Luba QC (Legal Action Group) see www.lag.org.uk

Court procedures and housing cases – a practitioner's guide Rita Parmer and Michael Parry (Shelter) see www.shelter.org.uk/publications

Shelter Guide: Mortgage arrears (Shelter) see www.shelter.org.uk/publications

Chapter 3

Guide to Housing Benefit and Council Tax Benefit John Zebedee, Martin Ward and Sam Lister (Shelter/CIH) see www.shelter.org.uk/publications

Shelter Guide: Housing benefit and local housing allowance (Shelter) see www.shelter.org.uk/publications

Welfare Benefits and Tax Credits Handbook (CPAG) see www.cpag.org.uk

Chapter 4

Repairs: Tenants' Rights Jan Luba QC and Stephen Knafler (Legal Action Group) see www.lag.org.uk

Shelter Guide: Getting repairs done (Shelter) see www.shelter.org.uk/publications

Shelter Guide: Gas and fire safety (Shelter) see www.shelter.org.uk/publications

Residential long leaseholders – a guide to your rights and responsibilities (CLG) see www.communities.gov.uk/publications/housing/residentiallongleaseholders

Chapter 5

Quiet Enjoyment 6th edition, Andrew Arden QC, David Carter and Andrew Dymond (Legal Action Group) see www.lag.org.uk

Fuel Rights Handbook (CPAG) see www.cpag.org.uk

Chapter 6

Shelter Guide: Relationship breakdown (Shelter) see www.shelter.org.uk/publications

Matrimonial Property and Finance Peter Duckworth (Oyez Longman)

Appendix 2: Useful contacts

Age Concern (England)
Astral House, 1268 London Road, London SW16 4ER
Tel: 0800 00 99 66
www.ageconcern.org.uk

Advisory Service for Squatters
Angel Alley, 84b Whitechapel High Street, Whitechapel
London E1 7QX
Tel: 0845 644 5814
www.squatter.org.uk

Association of Residential Letting Agents
Maple House, 53-55 Woodside Road, Amersham,
Bucks HP6 6AA
www.arla.co.uk

British Insurance Brokers Association
14 Bevis Marks, London EC3A 7NT
Members: 0844 77 00 266
Helpline: 0901 814 0015 (Call charges are 25p/min,
average call length 2–3min)
www.biba.org.uk

Broken Rainbow
Tel: 08452 604 460
www.broken-rainbow.org.uk

Building Societies Association
6th Floor, York House, 23 Kingsway, London WC2B 6UJ
Tel: 020 7437 0655
www.bsa.org.uk

Child Poverty Action Group
94 White Lion Street, London N1 9PF
Tel: 020 7833 4627 (advice agencies only)
www.cpag.org.uk

Citizens Advice
Myddelton House, 115–123 Pentonville Road, London N1 9LZ
Tel:020 7833 2181
www.adviceguide.org.uk

Commission for Local Administration in England
Local Government Ombudsman, 10th Floor, Millbank Tower,
Millbank, London SW1P 4QP
Tel: 0845 602 1983
www.lgo.org.uk

Community Development Foundation
Unit 5, Angel Gate, 320-326 City Road, London EC1V 2PT
Tel: 020 7833 1772
www.guide-information.org.uk

Community Legal Service Direct
Tel: 0845 345 4345
www.clsdirect.org.uk

Directgov
www.direct.gov.uk

Disability Alliance
Universal House, 88–94 Wentworth Street, London E1 7SA
Tel: 020 7247 8776
www.disabilityalliance.org

Equality and Human Rights Commission
Kingsgate House, 66–74 Victoria Street, London SW1E 6SW
Tel: 020 7215 8415
www.equalityhumanrights.com

Federation of Black Housing Organisations
Second Floor, 1 King Edwards Road, London E9 7SF
Tel: 020 8533 7053
www.fbho.org.uk

Gingerbread
255 Kentish Town Road, London NW5 2LX
Tel: 020 7428 5400
www.gingerbread.org.uk / www.oneparentfamilies.org.uk

Help the Aged
207–221 Pentonville Road, London N1 9UZ
Tel: 020 7278 1114
www.helptheaged.org.uk

HoDis (Research and campaigning group for the use and adaptation of accommodation for people with disabilities)
17 Priory Street, York YO1 6ET
Tel: 01904 653888

Home Information Packs
Home Ownership Policy Branch, Department for Communities and Local Government, 2/J9 Eland House, Bressenden Place, London, SW1E 5DU
Tel: 020 7944 4400
www.homeinformationpacks.gov.uk

Homeless Link
First floor, 10–13 Rushworth Street, London SE1 0RB
Tel: 020 7960 3010
www.homeless.org.uk

The Housing Corporation
149 Tottenham Court Road, London W1T 7BN
Tel: 0845 230 7000
www.housingcorp.gov.uk

The Housing Ombudsman Service
81 Aldwych, London WC2B 4HN
Tel: 020 7421 3800
www.ihos.org.uk

Housing Rights Service (NI)
4th Floor, Middleton Buildings, 10–12 High Street, Belfast BT1 2BA
Tel: 028 9024 5640
www.housingrights.org.uk

Immigration Advisory Service
County House, 190 Great Dover Street, London SE1 4YB
Tel: 020 7967 1200
www.iasuk.org

Joint Council for Welfare of Immigrants
115 Old Street, London EC1V 9JR
Tel: 020 7251 8708
www.jcwi.org.uk

Law Centres Federation
293–299 Kentish Town Road, London NW5 2TJ
Tel: 020 7428 4400
www.lawcentres.org.uk

Law Society
www.lawsociety.org.uk/choosingandusing/findasolicitor.law

Leasehold Advisory Service
31 Worship Street, London EC2A 2DX
Tel: 020 7374 5380
www.lease-advice.org

Legal Action Group
242 Pentonville Road, London N1 9UN
Tel: 020 7833 2931
www.lag.org.uk

Lesbian and Gay Switchboard
Tel: 020 7837 7324
www.llgs.org.uk

Lone Parent Helpline
Tel: 0800 018 5026
www.oneparentfamilies.org.uk

Mankind UK
PO Box 124, Newhaven, East Sussex BN9 9TQ
Tel: 0870 794 4124
www.mankinduk.co.uk

Men's Advice Line
1st Floor, Downstream Building, 1 London Bridge,
London SE1 9BG
Tel: 0808 801 0327
www.mensadviceline.org.uk

Multikulti
www.multikulti.org.uk

National Approved Letting Scheme
Tavistock House, 5 Rodney Road, Cheltenham GL50 1HX
Tel: 01242 581712
www.nalscheme.co.uk

National Association of Estate Agents
Arbon House, 6 Tournament Court, Edgehill Drive,
Warwick CV34 6LG
Tel: 01926 496800
www.naea.co.uk

National Debtline
Tel: 0808 808 4000
www.nationaldebtline.co.uk

National Family Mediation
Tel: 01392 271610
www.nfm.org.uk

National Mediation Centre
Tel: 01792 469626
www.dispute.co.uk

Office of Fair Trading
Fleetbank House, 2–6 Salisbury Square, London EC4Y 8JX
Tel: 020 7211 8000
www.oft.gov.uk

OFGEM (Office of Gas and Electricity Markets)
Tel: 0845 906 0708
www.ofgem.gov.uk / www.energywatch.org.uk

One Parent Families
See contact details for Gingerbread, above

Prison Advice and Care Trust
Suite C5, City Cloisters, 196 Old Street, London EC1V 9FR
Tel: 0808 808 2003
www.prisonadvice.org.uk

Public Services Ombudsman for Wales
1 Ffordd yr Hen Gae, Pencoed CF35 5LJ
Tel: 01656 641 150
www.ombudsman-wales.org.uk

Refuge
National Domestic Violence Helpline: 0808 200 0247
www.refuge.org.uk/www.womensaid.org.uk

Refugee Council
240–250 Ferndale Road, London SW9 8BB
Tel: 020 7346 6700
www.refugeecouncil.org.uk

Relate
Tel: 08451 304 016
www.relate.org.uk

Resource Information Service
Bramah House, 65–71 Bermondsey Street, London SE1 3XF
Tel: 020 7939 0641
www.ris.org.uk

Royal Association for Disability and Rehabilitation
12 City Forum, 250 City Road, London EC1V 8AF
Tel: 020 7250 3222
www.radar.org.uk

Royal Institution of Chartered Surveyors
RICS Contact Centre, Surveyor Court, Westwood Way,
Coventry CV4 8JE
Tel: 0870 333 1600
www.rics.org

Shelter
88 Old Street, London EC1V 9HU
Tel: 0808 800 4444
www.shelter.org.uk/adviceonline

More detailed information on housing law can be found on the
Shelter Legal subscription site www.shelter.org.uk/legal

UK Association of Letting Agents
59 Mile End Road, Colchester CO4 5BU
Tel: 01206 853741
www.ukala.org.uk

UK College of Family Mediators
Tel: 0117 904 7223
www.ukcfm.co.uk

Warm Front
The scheme manager administering Warm Front across England
is Eaga Partnership Ltd
Freepost Warm Front Team, 12054,
Newcastle Upon Tyne NE2 1BR
Tel: 0800 316 6011
www.eaga.co.uk

Which?
2 Marylebone Road, London, NW1 4DF
Tel: 020 7770 7000
www.which.co.uk

Women's Aid Federation
PO Box 391, Bristol BS99 7WS
Tel: 0808 200 0247
www.womensaid.org.uk

Index